INTIMATE
INNOVATION

Copyright Andrew Harrison 2013
ISBN 978-1-909847-00-2

INTIMATE INNOVATION

HOW OUR CAPACITY TO INNOVATE DEPENDS ON THE WAY WE RELATE

BY ANDREW HARRISON

Published by learning studio

DEDICATION, AND HOPE

I am always struck by the dedicatory preambles to books - I like to read them. They often seem warm and good natured, with a hint of the human behind the organised words . They have a distinctive tone to my ear. A tone in which…

- …we are all in it together….

- …you have no idea how much I needed the help of these people I am about mention…

- I have been so absorbed in this for the past xx years….I hope that this absorbs you…

- I am so glad that they still love me…even though I have been neglecting them while I have been writing this book, and making the ideas in this book make sense to me…

- …and I so hope that they make sense to you….

- …and I was so pleased that they made sense to the people I live with, the people I work with, the people I know…

- …and I am afraid of the loss of having finished it and sending it to you, so be gentle with it and take care of what I have made….

And then – usually – there is an abrupt shift of tone; the book begins proper. All the tender, searching, real nature of making something complex and organic, goes. It is there in the dedication, but not in the discourse. I hope that this is not such a book. I hope that some of that tone carries through.

This book is based on my last thirty years working – on work in many many organisations, special encounters with people at work, remarkable conversations at conferences (especially those of ISPSO). In the past few years several experiences have been especially significant: working with the OECD in Trento and Tunisia, Mandalah in Brazil, a course at Schumacher College in Devon, conversations with Tim Wood and Philip Boxer and David Armstrong. Being a father and step father has been a crucial component, given how families are systems, and how starting a new family and changing the nature of all of the existing family connections is – itself – a radical form of innovation. For Gwen, Sam and Harry, with love.

And none of it would have been possible – not now – without the compelling depth and vitality of knowing Sarah. To whom, without whom, by whom and with whom. I have had you in mind as I have written, you and the intimate marks you have made in and on me.

So, I hope you like it; I hope you all like it. I have had to do it anyway.

TABLE OF CONTENTS

Chapter one - Why intimate innovation?   1

- Core propositions   5
- Not about 'personal' relationships   7
- Innovation – so what?   9
- Saving ourselves from ourselves   13
- Ethics and intimacy   16

Chapter two - What is intimate innovation?   19

- 12+ versions of innovation   28
- Innovating through shared experiences   53
- In the here and now   57
- Dynamics, rather than method   62
- Implications of intimacy-in-innovation   64
- The conditions for intimate innovation   68

Chapter three - How does intimate innovation work? 73

- Our own experience of innovation   76
- Space and time   78
- When something is touching   80
- Disruption and betrayal   84
- Changing my mind   86
- Forms of vitality   88
- Compliance and consent   94
- Adoption   96
- Something social going on   100
- Surprise and stress   105
- Intimate regulation   107
- Inter-subjective dynamics   112
- Free association   114
- My internal marketplace   120

On our www site (www.intimate-innovation.co.uk), there is intimate innovation @ work in politics, business, economics, society, leadership and technology…join in the dialogue…

THE VOICE

I want to present a series of conjectures, inviting you into a kind of experience of reverie, or an experience of a kind of reverie. I am going to try and think about something with you.

Using conjectures as a structuring device might exaggerate and misrepresent the extent to which there are connections between each of the sections of these words-for-now; each section and each conjecture could 'stand alone'. Alternatively, there will be themes that emerge from both the conjectures and the way that they are organised – their sequencing, their differing length and tone, and the relationships that there are between them. I would be thrilled if one of the traces became a thread became a hunch became an idea for you...

Perhaps one could visualise this as a type of gallery – in which related but free-standing ideas are explored. I invite you to picture yourself walking round the gallery and considering the different conjectures as if they were pictures. It follows that the material could be organised in a different way.

The ideas of several authors have helped to shape this voice. Daniel Stern in his book *Forms of Vitality* (2010 page 3) writes:

'The idea of this book is to call attention to an aspect of human experience that remains largely 'hidden in plain view'. This is the experience of vitality. It is rarely talked about, yet vitality takes on many .... dynamic forms and permeates daily life, psychology, psychotherapy, and the arts'.

I have a similar purpose in mind in relation to intimacy and innovation. You couldn't argue that innovation is 'rarely talked about' – in some circles it is the major preoccupation. It is our experience of – and relation to – innovation though, that that is rarely talked about and is *'hidden in plain view'* in all walks of life, but particularly the world of work, business, organisations, and society.

Innovation is *'hidden in plain view'*, yet our experience of it – our relation to it – comes from 'left field'. Put more elegantly, by Ray Bradbury: *'The future comes from the periphery'*. And one of the ways in which we become aware of the periphery – for – us is through intimate relatedness.

As Frank Rose describes it in his book the *Art of Immersion* (2001), *'we are media'*. I suggest that the hypertext – that the linking dynamic of this experience of me-being-the-medium – is intimacy; and crucial in this linking dynamic is my *capacity* to be in such relation to myself and others.

Adam Phillips helps with this idea of *'capacity'*. In his *Fontana Modern Master on Winnicott* (1997 page 58) he discusses the idea of 'capacity' – widely used in Winnicott's work. Phillips suggests that 'capacity carries an *'...implication of stored possibility...'* and a *'...combination of the receptive and the generative (which) blurs the boundary between activity and passivity'*. In this sense, this book is about the capacity in us, in organisations, in systems – for innovation.

THE STRUCTURE

This book is structured into a series of themed chapters. They are overlapping and inter-connected (as you would expect); but there is less of an argument being made, than an emerging proposition being considered.

I am trying to 'look into' this topic with you; I am trying to make some suggestions, rather than 'tell' you anything. I believe in the potential power of the proposition, but I am far from sure of the implications. So, there is something of an opening[1] intended in this book. The three main sections are:

- why intimate innovation – in which I....review our 'hope' of innovation... its ethics, risks and the crucial role it plays in our kind of society; and begin to explore why the intimacy of innovation is of interest and value.

- what is intimate innovation – in which I... review some of the contemporary points of view on innovation; explore what I know about the experience of intimacy and its relation to innovation; and look at how this might augment some of the other, related views of innovation.

---

1. There is a www site (www.intimate-innovation.co.uk) to accompany this, a LinkedIN group (search for 'intimate innovation' within the LinkedIn groups' directory) for discussion threads.

- how does intimate innovation work – in which I....consider the dynamics of intimate innovation; and think about how the conditions for intimate innovation might be brought about and nurtured.

I have faced a challenge with the material that has gone into the making of this book. Some of it has come from conventional sources – books in the main, or print media of some kind. Where I can I have honoured those in foot notes and on the www site.

But much more – in volume – of the material has come from fragments of conversations with my intimates, www distributed videos (like RSAnimate, TED talks, IQsquared), blogs, newsprint etc

So on the www site there is a collection of sources – organised in ways which seem to make sense to me – but they are not all directly referenced to the text. In this sense, they are not footnotes. Neither are they resources – in the sense of learning 'resources' or 'tools'; they are fragments that have taken on sufficient form to provide the tension that is the structure of this proposition: that intimacy is the dna of innovation. We are all intimate innovators @ work.

CHAPTER 1

CHAPTER ONE : WHY INTIMATE INNOVATION?

I want to invite you to connect up some parts of your experience in a novel way; try out some ideas for size; work with them like actors would in rehearsal, or move them around on the page as if they were shapes and you were an artist. Listen to this dialogue. Speak it in your voice.

- something is happening to me – I am touched...

- you get through to me...I don't know what is happening, but something is happening...

- it feels good...it feels scary in a nice kind of way...

- you are under my skin...

- I see myself looking back at me...I am understood in a way that I did not understand myself...

- somehow ...how?...something is happening inside me...

- I am having an intimate experience with you...

- it seems to me that we are having an intimate experience... but, hang on a minute ... is this right?

- am I right? Is this what's going on?

- is this what is going on from your point of view?

- it seems to me to be what is going on from my point of view?

- but, hang on... I have just lost my earlier sense of what is my point of view?

- my point of view has changed...

- somehow you have become part of my point of view...you have changed me...

- have I changed you?

- some of this change I want....some of this change I sort of want...some of it I resist...what's that about?

- it feels as if this change wants me...

- where do I begin and end...I'm losing track...feeling edgy..

- what's going on?

Do you recognise this dialogue? Perhaps you have had a version of this with yourself, with real others, with imagined others – with significant others – and the dialogue may have added to the significance – it is certainly about 'significance'. And about the way in which new experience 'gets-to-you', gets@you.

CORE PROPOSITIONS

My contention in this book is that

- there are parallels between the processes of innovation that 'work'[2] and the experience of intimacy[3];

- that being innovative and being intimate are closely related. In this sense, to innovate is to be – at least in part, and to some extent – intimate; and to be intimate is to be innovative, or if not innovative, there is at least a possibility of something new in intimacy;

- to some extent all innovation involves a 'change-of-mind' – and yet we do not often see it as such; we dwell on the 'change-of-behaviour' interpretation of innovation – rather than recognise the *graffiti-wisdom* of 'change your mind and your ass will follow';

- in essence this is about how things-affect-you; about how you let someone (or something) else 'in'; or – in other words – how you 'take-on-board'; how you internalise;

- so I want to problematise the notion of 'buy in' (as in 'buy-into-an-innovation' or 'buy-into-a-change-programme') and propose that if

---

2. By 'work' I mean sticky, gain traction, make a difference, lead to change, re-new-all.
3. I am not going to explore if intimacy 'works'; that it 'works' is an ethical position in our time. However, in this book we are interested in the 'workings', the dynamics of intimacy and what that might tell us about innovation in values, point of view and behaviour. So we are interested in the ethics of the workings of intimacy.

you neglect intimacy, then 'buy-in' is experienced as a form of 'sell-out';

- part of how you create the capacity to internalise is through the co-created 'gap' between what is now, and a future, desired state;

- improvising helps with the creation of the capacity to experience this gap – intimacy helps with it, too;

- but I also want to share with you my sense of the 'day-to-day-ness' of this theme; how innovation (viewed from a more intimate perspective) is not a rare, or 'one-off' experience – but rather something that is taking place continually. I am constantly changing my mind, making my mind up (in different ways, in different combinations).

- I further suggest that there is a co-creation, a co-construction of meaning involved in this – and an assumption of a high degree of plasticity, in which we are all impressionable.

- finally, I want to share with you my surprise that these themes seem to be so little acknowledged – that they are there, 'hidden in plain view', in our day to day experience at work (and elsewhere). And yet rarely described or considered. Why might this be? I would go so far as to say that intimacy is a driver of innovation – and yet remains unexamined, as if we had a blind spot about it.

These are our core propositions about intimate innovation – as opposed to any-other-version-of-innovation.

NOT ABOUT 'PERSONAL' RELATIONSHIPS

This is not a book about 'personal' relationships – it is a book about innovation. Yet the evidence seems to suggest that it is the neglect of personal relationships and their intimate dynamic that helps to explain why attempts to innovate fail; and why – conversely – some attempts succeed.

Intimacy is business critical if you want to bring about lasting change.

In renaissance Venice, all of the contracts for trade were struck on the Rialto; as Steven Johnson discusses in *'Emergence'* (2001), the Ponte Vecchio in Florence served a similar purpose amongst gold and silversmiths. Many innovation theorists place huge emphasis on this 'clustering' phenomenon – like in Palo Alto, California; or Old Street, London.

Where the proliferation of connections, where the relationships between different people – with differing expertise and interests – and the nutrients of knowledge and freedom to associate (free association) with your neighbours – all lead to a proliferation of ideas. This is what I am after. This is an aspect of intimate innovation at work; an inter-play of what is different and those who are different.

This is all about how to relate to what and who is different – how to use difference to innovate. And – interestingly – some conjecture that the crucial people in these cultures[4] are the ones who 'move between' – the 'deal makers', the connectors, the brokers, the synthesisers who help to facilitate more, better, deeper, the early vulnerable stages of relationships, even of intimacy, maybe?

So far, I have introduced the 'intimate' half of our 'intimate innovation' pairing. Let's now turn to the 'innovation' dimension. But I don't want to stray into management 'talk' about innovation. I want to keep in mind what we have been trying to establish about

- the hidden-in-view, displayed below the surface quality of the intimate dynamic in innovation;

- the poly-dimensional, hyper-connected[5] quality of many many interactions all taking place in each moment;

- the sense I am developing in my over-lapping propositions that it is only through intimacy that the adoption of innovation can be optimized – in some essential sense, anything new has been made by more than one of us, made between us; and

- that there is something radical and urgent about getting better acquainted with these themes, having a closer, better delineated knowledge of our own capacity for innovation and how our sense of our own and others' intimacy may help or hinder that process.

---

4. Interesting word in this context – since bacteria proliferate in a 'culture' (few more intimate organisms than bacteria); and we so often associate ideas of 'culture change' with innovation.

5. I find this so hard to visualise and describe to you – but the images assembled by Manuel Lima www.visualcomplexity.com go some way to convey this sense of infinite connectedness.

INNOVATION – SO WHAT?

So, why this preoccupation – in particular – with innovation; since we could be talking about intimate marketing, intimate project management, intimate leadership etc etc? There are several reasons…

First, innovation is often seen as an 'expert' function - you innovate and I implement 'your' innovation – it is seen as a quality of individuals or a by-product of particular behaviours, rather than a property of the system. Indeed, many of the prevailing theories of innovation and its diffusion are based on a dominant metaphor of 'spread' - out from a place where innovation has taken place (and a group of people who were innovators), into 'empty' space where it has not yet happened; and in that space, there will be resistance to its spread.

I want to challenge – or at least augment – this view with the proposition that there will only ever be adoption if some kind of consent is involved. Compliance and adoption are incompatible. Therefore, I need to be intimate in how I adopt. So, rather than the dominant metaphor being 'spread', I suggest it needs to be 'relate' – on the understanding that 'attention' in relationship has a shaping influence.

Second, it is often seen as a 'special' or privileged 'state of being' or 'state of mind', something that is done, that you do – under particular conditions, when it is needed. It is not a permanent state, way of being, or way of seeing the world. It is not a function of all relating.

I want to take issue with this: I am 'changing my mind' all of the time[6]. And discoveries in neuroscience and the use we make use of mirror neurons mean that in a profound, matter-of-fact way, we are constantly 'making up' our minds all of the time through our relationships with one another. The ambiguity of the notion of 'making up' is evocative of

- constructing something – including the possibility of the 'gap' between what is and what could be
- resolving a contradiction
- healing a rift

….yet implies something of falsehood, as in 'I made up that story'; and in such an act I made an irresponsible use of difference.

Third, what can we do to understand the ways in which innovations provoke an immune response, something akin to tissue rejection? Ideas get killed off, as they enter the system. People gather round them is if they were anti-bodies around a wound or an infection, starving them of nutrients to heighten stress and lead to dormancy. The phenomenon of 'immunity to change'[7], and the uses of organising as a social defence against innovation is comparable to a process of preservation, or

---

6. We will discuss this dynamic in the next section, inspired by Daniel Stern in his *Forms of Vitality*; where he evokes a sense of the constant 'hum' of interactions in daily life, each intimate, each part of the capacity to innovate.
7. See www.uknow.gse.harvard.edu/leadership/LP3-4.html for a discussion of this idea based on '*Immunity to Change*' Robert Kegan and Lisa Laskow Lahey, Harvard University Press (2009).

protection – not against competition from the outside, or demands from those whose needs and wants your organisation avowedly exists to meet. The 'competition' comes from you – when this happens we could call competition 'resistance' or 'loss of identity'.

It seems to be a protection against the 'new' (since it threatens the continuity of my intimate identity) from outside me, yet also comes from within me (since if I can maintain my repression of alternative ways of being intimate for the moment, I can maintain the illusion that the uncertainty of the future is reduced to a re-mould of now). This suggests I become my own version of the Mobius strip – where the inside and outside are continuous.

I convert the future into something predictable. This familiarity[8] seems to be part of something almost akin to an *aesthetic of 'being stuck'* – I find a beautiful consolation in not being able to do anything other than that which I am used to doing – with the familiar consequences for me, and for others. In their book, *Immunity to Change* (2009), Kegan and Lahey describe this kind of state as 'optimal conflict', in which (page 54) we experience:

- the *persistent* experience of some frustration, dilemma, life puzzle, quandary, or personal problem that is…

- perfectly designed to cause us to *feel the limits* of our current way of knowing…

- in some sphere of our living that we *care about*, with…

---

8. In a former era, 'a familiar' carried the same meaning as 'an intimate'; people to whom to a degree I am close.

- *sufficient supports* so that we are neither overwhelmed by the conflict nor able to escape or defuse it.

My contention is that one of the ways – maybe the only way – of moving beyond this particular version of optimal conflict is through some kind of intimate relating, and in the very DNA of that relating is the latent potential for innovation.

Finally, there is near universal recognition that economic growth depends on innovation; it is our fantasy panacea....we are all party to a popular discourse in which we share conjectures of resolving almost inconceivable dilemmas around a shared optimism in the endless efficacy of innovation. It will be what helps us to;

- avert the consequences of global warming;

- solve welfare crises;

- mitigate world poverty by innovating better, faster, more lastingly ... and so on and so on...

- and you could also argue that we most urgently need to innovate around values, and a sense of community.

The role of innovation in the paradigm of capitalism is critically important to our theme. Theorists of globalization link together freedom of movement of goods, and services, labour and capital; higher and higher levels of skills & education; the importance of cost differentials etc etc. And the activity that is creating value in this world view is innovation – because through the application of new ideas, the empowering cycle of globalisation will be renewed.

SAVING OURSELVES FROM OURSELVES

In a 2011[9] edition of *Management Today*, in the aftermath of the then financial crisis, there was an article called 'Saving Capitalism from Itself'. I can't resist conjecturing on the use of this phrase – when one says, let us say, of a friend or acquaintance, 'he or she needs to saved from themselves', it is usually a knowing reference to a blind-spot which we can see and they cannot. As such, it is a comment on another's shortcoming in their relation to themselves. It is an assessment of their capacity for self-knowledge. It comments on their capacity to be intimate with themselves. So, capitalism has to be blind to its own shortcomings in order to persist; so do I. That is why I need you. This is how intimacy saves us from ourselves.

In the *Management Today* piece, there were four points of view from opinion formers, who were in four different ways proposing distinct ways of innovating to create 'new value', and a new set of relationships between the various interests in the capitalist system.

These were presented as responses to a critique of the 'fish-rots-from-the-head' kind about capitalism, collapsing under the weight of its own contradictions (Marx). The article was contextualised with remarks from Roger Martin, author of *Fixing the Game* (2011) – itself an ambiguous phrase encapsulating assumptions about 'gaming', 'repair', and 'rules known only to a few': fixers don't only repair – they also satisfice, making deals behind the scenes to make things work, for now, for them, and those whose interests they serve.

9. 23rd August 2011

This – in itself – could be seen as the antithesis to the intimate values we are trying to reveal.

The article carries its article of faith about 'human ingenuity' all the way through, with an exposition of the following positions:

- shared value– (rather than 'share' value) as a by product of 'deep reform' from Michael Porter;
- thick value – (rather than 'thin' value) from Umair Haque;
- reinvention of (management) nimbleness – from Gary Hamel – a version of Lewin's formulation that learning needs to be either at the same rate as, or faster than, the rate of change in order to have any impact; and
- 'deep introspection' to re-establish leadership – from Dominic Barton.

In pointing to conceptual ways ahead, these use the vocabulary of intimacy – 'sharing' and 'value' and 'nimble attunement' and 'deep introspection' – all of these being aspects of the version of intimacy we are exploring.

Their theories of recovery and redemption – under which capitalism is to be saved from itself – require an encounter of the self with the other which is intimate, in essence. Indeed, Umair Haque visualises a world in which there is a kind of 'global intimacy' (my phrase) – during the Arab Spring, he tweeted, 'that's you in Syntagma Square: you just don't know it yet.'

And this is reminiscent of the 'revenge of the nomad[10]' version of the Shengen Agreement in Europe, where the free movement of people within the European Union has shocked the establishment and the tribal identities of all of us; and exposed the extent to which trying to relate to difference without intimacy as a mediating dynamic leads to rupture and crisis.

'Haque depicts a business future made by individual decisions. The concepts of 'thick' and 'thin' value outlined in his book and his direct calls to action to put eudaemonia (wellbeing) and meaning at the centre of both enterprise and consumption are a combination that may prove vital for the next phase of capitalist evolution,' says Management Today

Central to their thinking about the crisis, is a critique of 'ownership' (who owns what under capitalism, ironically discussed in terms of 'shares', as if sharing and plough shares were under consideration).

But what I own of myself and what I am prepared to share with you – what I am able to share with you (without loss of identity) – what I might be tricked into sharing with you – what I consent to share with you – what I collude in sharing with you – what I am seduced into sharing with you - all of these are (in part) questions of intimacy. As is the reverse, where you may seduce me, you may collude with me, you may trick me.

Both sides need to be in dynamic relatedness in order for there to be the possibility of intimacy; but in this global, intimate context

---

10. Idea from Sigmund Baumann, part of his 'liquid modernity' theme.

this familiar, close, tender state of being is combined with a kind of poly dimensional connectedness, where relationships – of all kinds – proliferate. The contemporary challenge is – in part – how to remain intimately related to any, whilst connected to so many.

ETHICS AND INTIMACY

In May 2012[11], Malcolm Bull reviewed a book by Stephen Gardiner, *Perfect Moral Storm: the ethical tragedy of climate change* (2013). This review considers – as a by product of its argument about morality and climate change – how the realisation of intimate connection leads to innovation; in this case in ethics. Malcolm Bull writes:

'Adam Smith once noted that we are less troubled by the prospect of a hundred million people dying as a result of an earthquake in some distant location than of losing our little finger, but would nevertheless be horrified by the idea we might allow them to die in order to save it.'

This is familiar stuff – journalists and media figures often seem to expect to work on this assumption; 'local' news seems to exist because of it. But the ethical challenge of climate change presents significant dilemmas to us, and our assumptions about 'how to do good, and act well'. As Malcolm Bull suggests:

---

11. Available from www.lrb.co.uk/v34/n10/malcolm-bull/what-is-the-rational-response [Accessed 3 June 2012].

'Climate change .... places unprecedented demands on our moral imagination. Almost every little thing we do contributes to our carbon footprint, which increases greenhouse gases, which could in turn ultimately threaten hundreds of millions of lives in some remote time and place – the uncertainty only adding to the sublime awfulness of our responsibilities.'

Almost every little thing we do contributes to our carbon footprint – so there are millions and millions of little steps making up our footprint. These inflections are the words in this book. The messages you text. The switches you flick. The corners you drive round. The planes you sit in.

Our actions – in their almost microscopic detail, and molecular, florid, profusion – are going to have an impact on people not yet born, who will be intimate with others after we are dead. The unprecedented demands made on our moral imagination include caring for people we will never know who do not yet exist, and who will try to live in places we will never go.

And then Malcolm Bull goes on to say:

'... climate change does not tempt us to be less moral than we might otherwise be; it invites us to be more moral than we could ever have imagined....Climate ethics is not morality applied but morality discovered, a new chapter in the moral education of mankind. It may tell us things we do not wish to know (about democracy, perhaps), but the future development of humanity may depend on what, if anything, it can teach us'.

That phrase – 'climate ethics is not morality applied but morality discovered' – captures something I am reaching for in the re-imagining of the nature of innovation and our relation to innovative experiences. I am suggesting that the linking of intimacy to innovation moves us in a realm that is more than applied – or where the specificity and power of the application could be maintained and amplified in all contexts.

Intimate innovation is innovation re-imagined; innovation re-discovered.

CHAPTER 2

CHAPTER TWO: WHAT IS INTIMATE INNOVATION?

In the past few years, I have become aware of some of the emergent models of innovation that either have gained or are gaining traction.

They come and go. They are all trying to add to the suggestive store of responses to the questions of, 'what is innovation?', 'how does innovation work?', 'how do you make it stick?' Here are 12+ examples which have made more 'noise', and around which there has been more dialogue, as far as I can tell. These are:

Type	...by which I understand....
Disruptive innovation – first appeared in 1997. Clayton Christensen in his book *The Innovator's Dilemma* (Harvard Business School Press).	Disruptive innovation will often have characteristics that traditional customer segments *'may not want'*, at least initially. Such innovations will appear as cheaper, simpler and even of inferior quality if compared to existing products, but some marginal or new segment will value them.

Type	...by which I understand....
User innovation – original thinking by Eric von Hippel; appears in some ways to be a variant on open innovation.	User innovation is based on the idea that much innovation (especially in technology), is developed by users of products and services, rather than producers. Linked idea of 'sticky' information – which is high cost, and hard to access for the developer; but relatively accessible to users.
Crowd sourcing – *Wired* journalist, Geoff Howe, coined this phrase in 2006. Superceded by idea of 'insourcing', where 'deep collaboration' is developed between all/any parties.	'Hobbyists, part-timers, and dabblers suddenly have a market for their efforts, as smart companies in industries as disparate as pharmaceuticals and television discover ways to tap the latent talent of the crowd. The labour isn't always free, but it costs a lot less than paying traditional employees. It's not outsourcing; it's crowd sourcing'.
Frugal innovation - Inspired by the experience of frugal entrepreneurs in developing countries, like India.	This is a variant on user – led and disruptive innovation under which public and private services and products are provided in radically different ways. They lead to huge improvements in access to services at relatively little cost – therefore, frugal.

Type	...by which I understand....
Open innovation – idea introduced by Henry Chesbrough in 2003.	An approach to innovation under which organisations open themselves to a freer flow of information from suppliers and customers as partners in order to promote the proliferation of ideas, and to give them more access to 'sticky' information. In effect, they get closer and more involved with one another.
Cloud innovation – a form of open innovation platform.	A 'space' (if a cloud can be a space) in which innovation is under-pinned by open source software. There are versions of this being developed, including (from Microsoft) a 'private' cloud; Apple recently launched 'iCloud' – for which we could read 'intimacycloud'.
Asymmetric innovation[12] – a set of ideas developed by Phillip Boxer.	This is an approach to innovation in an organisational ecosystem in which you try to take power to the edge of the organisation so that the needs of the customer or patient are met in 'their-particular-context-of use'. This approach to innovation is set in its own paradigm; and provides a critique of 'adoption'.

12. This is one aspect of a much wider set of analytics designed to help see what is going on in complex organisational settings. It is especially powerful in making sense of healthcare innovation demands. See www.asymmetricleadership.com

Type	...by which I understand....
Soft innovation – rapid innovative change in the aesthetics of products and services.	Pioneered in papers from NESTA[13], this perspective on innovation stresses changes is aesthetics, rather than changes in technology as a source of innovation. In particular if the aesthetic change has some significant economic dimension. It is about product and process re-design – so considers fashion and low budget airlines (because the 'aesthetic[14]' of air travel has changed).
Personalisation – this is widely present in technology, and service system design. It is an example of system-wide soft innovation.	Based on the idea that the user is the best judge of how to specify what they need; in effect, they *combine* the product or service from a 'warehouse' which you provide. The reform of Adult Social Care Services in the UK (where the beneficiary and their carer 'commission' their own care from a 'personal budget); and iTunes and the APP store are examples of this trend.

13. The National Endowment for Science Technology and the Arts. See www.nesta.org.uk

14. This has interesting implications – as if 'aesthetics' and 'experience' were synonyms. This lends real, intimate force to the interest in 'user-experience', 'user inter-face', 'brand values' and 'brand experience'. My experience of your service, or product, or care pathway creates value for me if it is felt to be 'my' experience.

Type	...by which I understand....
Creative destruction – a term coined by Shumpeter as part of his theorising about the behaviour of companies who innovate.	This is an 'old hat' notion that has been woven into the work of Austrian and neo-conservative economists. It has been a driver (and un-examinable assumption) of UK public and economic policy ever since Mrs Thatcher was Prime Minister. Powerfully linked to the idea of 'entrepreneurship' (itself under-pinned by a kind of intimate economics). It is embedded in the 'fascist aesthetic[15]' of the UK (2014) coalition government.
Biomimicry[16] – (from *bios*, meaning life, and *mimesis*, meaning to imitate) is a design discipline that seeks sustainable solutions by emulating nature's time-tested patterns and strategies, e.g., a solar cell inspired by a leaf.	The core idea is that Nature, 'imaginative' (or at least resourceful) by necessity, has already solved many of the problems we are grappling with: energy, food production, climate control, non-toxic chemistry, transportation, packaging, and a whole lot more. This version of innovation began to be 'described' in the 1990s (having been a way of 'learning' or 'being inspired by nature' for millennia).

15. Fascist to the extent that the 'futurists' in 20th century Italy were so – reifying speed, and destruction as a source of beauty and creativity. Mussolini's politics and particular cult (brand) of leadership expressed this set of values. As such, fascism was an example of 'soft innovation' in politics in so far as it celebrated the aesthetic of 'creative destruction'.

16. Thanks to www.asknature.org/article/view/what_is_biomimicry for this

Type	...by which I understand....
Conscious innovation – the self-styled approach to innovation, developed and in use, by Mandalah Global since 2006.	They stress that innovation is a 'process', rather than a 'task' or a 'project'. This is not unusual – many, if not most, approaches to innovation stress the 'process'. What is unusual about Mandalah's conscious innovation is the mix of influences and values from which they build their process. In a profound way, their 'conscious' stance is opposed to a process of 'unthinking' innovation.
12+ - we can add to these examples, freely....	...there are examples of different approaches surfacing into my view again and again on the www (for example, while editing this, I came across Frans Johanssons' *Medici Effect* (2004) - arguing that innovation comes from 'crossover' influences between fields and disciplines) ....and ... • I wonder what the proliferating of approaches means? • Why so many? • Why with such fine distinctions between them?

My contention is that none of these ways of understanding innovation are complete unless you take account of the dynamics of intimacy.

I want to add to this menu of interpretations and approaches – I want to add in 'intimate innovation' – not as a competing idea, but as a way of describing the under-lying dynamic of all of these approaches; as a way of trying to get to the deep(er) depth of what-is-going-on in systems. I include the nuanced inflections of our systemic relationships with one another; our own intimacy. In the qualities of that capacity, lies the capacity to innovate, continually. In the sub-sections that follow, I discuss each of these approaches in some more detail.

DISRUPTIVE INNOVATION

...questions, comments, conjectures....from the point of view of our propositions...

A disruptive innovation helps create a new market and value network, and eventually goes on to disrupt an existing market and value network (over a few years or decades), displacing an earlier technology. The term is used to describe innovations that improve a product or service in ways that the market does not expect, typically first by designing for a different set of consumers in the new market and later by lowering prices in the existing market.

In contrast to *disruptive* innovation, a sustaining innovation does not create new markets or value networks but rather only evolves existing ones with better value, allowing the firms within to compete against each other's sustaining improvements. Sustaining innovations may be either "discontinuous" (i.e. "transformational" or "revolutionary") or "continuous" (i.e. "evolutionary"). It deals in *direct value* to the customer. It does not try to relate to sectoral, or systemic change.

Disruptive innovations, on the other hand, will often have characteristics that traditional customer segments may not want, at least initially. Such innovations will appear as cheaper, simpler and even with inferior quality if compared to existing products, but some marginal or new segment will value it; or even existing customers will see the *indirect value* in it. There is often greatest resistance to disruptive innovation from *established producers*.

Our earlier reflections on the dynamic so intimacy are interesting here. My intimate, inner life has a quality that is more like the churn of the disk drive industry, or the life cycle of fruit flies. My emotions, what I apprehend, what I avoid, that which I am oblivious to, or protecting myself from – all of these are part of the 'quiet storm' of emotions and sense data that form my intimate weather system.

Could there be a version of disruptive innovation that re-locates the sectoral change, in me, or you? In our intimate selves, where we need to sustain our identity (and therefore resist change). If I need to keep 'me' going, there is a risk that any innovation that jeopardizes the enduring continuity of my identity will be deeply disruptive. I will resist change, because the-trade-sector-of-myself-at-work, the industry that is me, my industriousness is changing faster than I can apprehend.

And the equivalent of the life cycle of fruit flies or the rate at which disc drives increase in power as they reduce in cost – this evolving proliferation, this torrent, all these interactions and the waste they generate – what is their intimate equivalent? Trauma? Crisis? Loss? This disruptive dynamic is equivalent to some aspects of the dynamic of intimate relating.

USER INNOVATION

...questions, comments, conjectures....from the point of view of our propositions...

User innovation is based on the observation that many products and services are actually developed or at least refined, by users, in their own context of use, developing innovations which are then moved back into the supply network. Arguably, the need to do this arises from the fact that products & services are developed to meet the widest possible need; when individual users face problems that the majority of consumers do not, they have no choice but to develop their own modifications to existing products, or entirely new products, to solve their issues. To the extent this is needed, it is evidence – to some degree – that my particular needs have not been met.

Perhaps the work that users do is far from grudging. Perhaps it is a way of intensifying their experience of the product or service, making it fit the shape of their experience and use, more closely. Makes it more intimate to me, as a user; indeed, re-defines me from the relative passivity of 'user' into the more active co-creator of the product or service.

Often, user innovators will share their ideas with manufacturers and / or service designers in the hope of having them produce the product, a process called 'free revealing'. What am I doing when I reveal freely, when I am being freely revealed? Sounds pretty close to a mode of intimacy to me.

The thick, hard to reach, valuable information about users that is 'sticky' information is in effect intimate information, or information about intimacy – know to the user, but very hard to capture and aggregate; not known to the producer without the users' consent and active involvement. Again, intimacy is written all over this idea.

Many organisations are developing business and service models to which user innovation is intrinsic. By definition, it is at the core of 'open source' software architecture. It is also intrinsic to the world of Apps. It is increasingly a feature of health care systems[17], where professionals are supporting the patient and carer in developing a more active relationship to their (often long-term) condition. A kind of user innovation is central to mental health therapies, where one could argue the whole challenge is to get the user more (and differently) involved in their own condition management. There is a sense in which user innovation is about 'getting me back to myself', getting me back into a co-creative relationship with myself as user.

Language is the perfect example of an intimate user innovation: with this system, within its architecture, I can say anything I want, and I am in a permanent process of modification, and sense making. Lovers develop private languages[18] – or so it seems to those outside their intimacy.

---

17. There seems to be a near universal principle that if I am involved in my own care, it is more likely to be effective. I have developed an intimate relationship to my symptomology; I look after myself and my relationship to myself; often, in doing so, my symptoms change.

18. Development of a private language can often be the prelude to innovation – a way of bringing something new into being.

CROWD SOURCING

...questions, comments, conjectures....from the point of view of our propositions...

Crowd sourcing (in essence) is not a new idea. The Longitude Prize (in the 18th century) and the development of the OED (in the 19th century) were crowd sourced innovations.

In coining the term of "crowd sourcing", Jeff Howe indicated some common categories of crowd sourcing that can be used effectively in the commercial world. Some of these web-based crowd sourcing efforts include crowd voting, wisdom of the crowd, crowdfunding, microwork, and inducement prize contests. This is not an exhaustive list – but it gives a flavour.

Under 'implicit' crowdsourcing, users do not necessarily know they are contributors, yet can still be very effective in completing certain tasks. Rather than users actively participating in solving a problem or providing information, implicit crowd sourcing involves users doing another task entirely where a third party gains information for another topic based on the user's actions. Club cards from supermarkets are an example of this, where the sticky information of your buying habits are aggregated up into a marketing and promotion profile.

Google's business model is based on this. They mine one's search history and websites in order to discover keywords for ads, spelling corrections, and finding synonyms. In this way, users are unintentionally helping to modify existing systems, such as Google's ad words.

Commentators (like Daniel Soar[19]) describes Google's way of learning as being like a baby's brain - an omnivorous sponge that was always getting smarter from the information it soaked up. Like a baby, Google uses what it hears to learn about the workings of human language, and – in particular – it learns from the mistakes we make as we 'search' its knowledge bank.

A baby's neurological relation to the world (of its mother, of sensation) is the epitome of intimacy. Google's relation to our search habits is comparably intimate. As Daniel Soar says, 'It knows'…all about me and you.

Eric Schmidt[20] conjectures that what people want is for Google to tell them what to do next is – in effect – a fantasy (or ominously perhaps, a business strategy) under which I will be so involved with Google, so closely connected, that I give up my own volition. I am developing a disordered attachment to my own means of communication with the world.

And crowd sourcing is an embodiment of this: so many more people to be close to, so many connections to make – yet in doing so, I am unwittingly providing the sticky information what will tie me to Google (or whoever). This is the vortex of one way of being intimate.

---

19. Daniel Soar: www.lrb.co.uk/v33/n19/daniel-soar/it-knows.
20. Discussed in Bryan Appleyard's *The Brain is Wider that the Sky* www.bryanappleyard.com.

FRUGAL INNOVATION

...questions, comments, conjectures....from the point of view of our propositions...

This way of seeing innovation is 'breaking news' (in 2012) – and interestingly is based on a radical re-definition of the dependency between the West and developing economies; challenging the imperial notions of one way innovation and knowledge transfer.

'Jugaad', innovators have a mindset that encapsulates several attitudes and practices, including the ability to seek opportunity in adversity, do more with less, think and act flexibly, keep things simple, include the margin, and follow the heart.

Jaideep Prabhu describes: 'the fruits, of 'jugaad' innovation include the $2000 Tata Nano car, $50 Aakash tablet PC, 1 cent/minute mobile phone calls, £500 electrocardiography (ECG) machines (and $1 ECG scans), $25 water purifier, $70 fridge that runs on batteries, and so on. They also include radical models of scaleable welfare care, for a fraction of the assumed costs in the West. Improved 'access' seems to be a driving idea.

Specifically, *jugaad* innovators are resilient, frugal, adaptable, inclusive, empathetic and passionate. All these traits help them to compete and succeed in the complex world of emerging markets; and all these traits are dimensions of our propositions about intimate innovation.

There is a move in 'austerity' Britain to find some Delhi 'drive', as a way of reforming public services; and setting aside a cynical interpretation of politicians' motives for this call, at its heart it is a call to alter our relationship with, the, state – and make it more of a relationship with 'our' state.

The eco-economist, Gunter Pauli, leader of the blue economy, is himself frugal & intimate in the kinds of business proposal and innovations he promotes. He regularly posts 'pop up' business propositions, each one of which redefines our relationship with resources and the value of waste; most of which are based on multiple revenue streams. There is something inspiring in linking the idea of 'our state' with a re-conceptualising of the value of what we waste.

OPEN INNOVATION

...questions, comments, conjectures....from the point of view of our propositions...

In 1997, Eric Raymond, writing about the open source software movement, coined the term *the cathedral and the bazaar*. The cathedral represented the conventional method of employing a group of experts to design and develop software (though it could apply to any large-scale creative or innovative work); the bazaar represented the open source approach, with its interactive, traded, patterned chaos.

This idea has been amplified by a lot of people, notably Don Tapscott and Anthony D. Williams in their book Wikinomics. Eric Raymond himself is also quoted as saying that 'one cannot code from the ground up in bazaar style. One can test, debug, and improve in bazaar style, but it would be very hard to originate a project in bazaar mode.' In the same vein, Raymond is also quoted as saying[21], 'The individual wizard is where successful bazaar projects generally start'.

NESTA in the UK has developed its own version of the idea, seeing each enterprise as sitting at 'the centre of an ecosystem, producing new value from its links with others.' NESTA describes open innovation as 'a new way of strengthening these links, making them more productive, efficient, and long-lasting.'

---

21. www.eclipse.org/org/foundation/membersminutes/20070920MembersMeeting/07.09.12-Eclipse-Open-Innovation.pdf.

NESTA supports its work in this field with an ethnographic approach to evaluation which helps it to get at the experience of innovation in the specific context of its application. They have developed two styles of open innovation – 'discover' and 'jam' – which contain contrasting ingredients (competitive & co-operative; inductive & deductive; trusted mediator & joint venturing).

In reviewing the material, I get the impression that the dynamic of this open innovation process is a mixture of the closed and open; the tight and loose; the independent and dependent – as if the process had a pulse, or beat to it. All of the case studies that NESTA feature speak of this mix of 'focus' and 'closeness', of something being prepared as-it- is-worked-on; indeed the working on and the preparing are the same process. As if one were refining.

The 100%open business models (developed at NESTA) describe six principles which centre around the notion that ideas are worthless (or at least worth-less than is usually assumed) because it is conversations that lead to relationships that lead to transactions. And I would add, that the whole of this cycle is a form of intimacy.

CLOUD INNOVATION

...questions, comments, conjectures....from the point of view of our propositions...

Cloud innovation is a type of open innovation – a hybrid of crowd sourcing – in which digital platforms provide an environment in which collaboration is facilitated and supported. The significant issue in relation to our theme is that it is in essence an infrastructure of relationships supported by technology, designed to create a new set of conditions for innovation.

Charles Leadbetter[22] discusses cloud innovation in terms of 'many-to-many' transformations – it has some resemblance to frugal innovation, in that low cost|high impact is the aim.

Part of the attraction of this innovation concept is the potential capacity of technology when applied to social[23] problems and needs. Indeed, the overtones of the concept of 'cloud' are social – *we are in this together.*

The upbeat prognosis for cloud culture and cloud innovation stresses how investment by one party in the development of – say

---

22. Social Innovation Global Academy Bilbao, April 2011. Sponsored by Young Foundation see here for more of similar material www.youngfoundation.org/publications.

23. One of the market leaders in cloud computing applications, HP, has an Office of Global Social Innovation which is using technology to support solutions to social problems www8.hp.com/us/en/hp-information/social-innovation/social-responsibility.html.

– a technology solution, will be available to all users of the cloud. This will promote use of shared resources and help foster 'cloud communities' of innovators.

Threats to the cloud culture of innovation appear to the threefold: rearguard action by the traditional media; government control of the cloud; and cloud capitalists – Google docs etc, iCloud – and there are substantial concerns over privacy. However, one of the central benefits of 'cloud innovation' is that users have access to an environment in which they can configure some kind of 'on-demand-self-service'. This is the basic appeal of iTunes and Kindle Publishing, for example.

One finds a similar trend in the use of iGoogle technology – where I can design the content of my own 'front page' on (for example) my local council's www site (so whenever I log on, I – first – get access to what matters most to me). Or in thinking about training and education – where rather than 'a curriculum', one gets access to various combinations of 'granular' learning experiences.

This notion of 'on demand self service' implies a form of intimacy – a matching of experience to self and self to experience, based on a process of micro interactions. But some of the features of intimacy in a crowd might well apply to innovation in the cloud, where we are only able to make fleeting relationships.

ASYMMETRIC INNOVATION

...questions, comments, conjectures....from the point of view of our propositions...

I have been introduced to the ideas under asymmetric innovation by Phillip Boxer, drawing on an eclectic range of sources (from Lacan to warfare). In essence, the asymmetry comes from the challenges of relating to demand that comes from all directions – demand that is multi-sided. And how does an 'enterprise' respond without pretending that this is not actually the case? And in the way that asymmetric warfare has shown, 'context is everything[24]'. Part of Phillip Boxer's insight is that the 'context-of-use' of the customer or patient is everything – indeed is part of the source of the multi-sidedness.

The ways of analysing that Phillip has developed are intended to support leaders in an environment of asymmetric demands, where situational judgements, exceptions, variety, differences – all of these are more like the facts-of-leadership-life than predictability, balance, controls, planning. He calls this *asymmetric leadership*.

As an asymmetric leader you are likely to be working with some combination of:

- customers' escalating demands within increasingly complex contexts;

---

24. Also central to Malcolm Gladwell's theory of 'Tipping Points'.

- the challenges of personalisation & individualisation by networks of providers;

- aligning through-life support and condition management for the customer across organisational boundaries;

- reducing duplication and eliminating waste, whilst increasing the emphasis on early intervention to secure long-term benefits; and

- trying to improve outcomes, especially in the case of complex needs.

So all that you do needs to become agile – in the same way that weapon systems need (now) to adapt their capability to a wide variety of theatres of war, and be capable of deployment by military men and women in a 'front line' which is no longer a 'line' (but a storm of interactions, all deadly). The implications of this include:

Developing governance which is 'horizontal' not 'vertical'; investigating 'wedges' of demand that cut through conventional, stratified delivery; seeing leadership itself as an 'economy' in which power is exchanged; operating across a whole ecosystem of organisations and services; expanding the understanding of alignment of services to relate to user – need throughout the life of their condition (with massive consequences for understanding costs, return on investment, pricing); and the growing significance of technology – enabled, 'platform' enterprises.

Moving power to the edge of your organisation where your customers interact with you in their own-very-own 'context of use' is at the core of this way of seeing innovation. It is as if every demand is unique[25]; how I consume is as much me as my signature or my idiom. My demands are (intimate) intimations. As such, the concept of 'adoption' in innovation thinking is re-imagined as 'alignment'.

---

25. See New York Times 32 Innovations that will change your tomorrow for a fascinating instance of this – we all put our phone to our ear in unique ways, as distinct as fingerprints. Your body will be your log-in. www.nytimes.com/interactive/2012/06/03/magazine/innovations-issue.html.

SOFT INNOVATION

...questions, comments, conjectures....from the point of view of our propositions...

NESTA define 'soft innovation 'as change of an aesthetic nature in a service or product which are economically significant. It contrasts, technology, with, aesthetics, to distinguish this mode of innovation from the dominant technology-focused discourses. The distinction made here between aesthetics and technology is an interesting one to us. Arguably *aesthetics is a technology* if and when you view innovation as an intimate relationship. When one speaks of the 'aesthetic' of an experience one is speaking of how it 'works' on you.

Soft innovation mainly concerns product and service differentiation; significantly, soft innovation may involve reductions in price if prices falls more than perceived quality (as in budget airlines).

Many models of innovation tend to assume (often implicitly) that innovation must be vertical – all users will prefer the new product or service at a given price because it is inherently better than the former product or service (or at least presented as such). This ignores two other possibilities:

- horizontal innovation where some consumers may prefer the new and others the old, when they are priced at a similar amount; and

- vertical innovation which does not involve an improvement in quality but may involve a lower price.

Soft innovation is often present in market sectors (like budget airlines, fashion, publishing and creative industries) where product and service life cycles are very short, and where there is huge 'churn' in content as the forms of distribution proliferate. Intellectual property[26] is a major factor in markets where soft innovation is a significant driver. Two factors are of further importance:

- rivalry: the impact of one person's ownership (of a product) on another person's enjoyment (of the same product); and

- excludability: the ease with which a product owner or supplier can limit or control ownership by others.

These final points suggest that part of the dynamism of soft innovation comes from the extent to which it can engender and maintain envy. Adapting Melanie Klein's formulations about the dynamics of intimate relationships between children and their parents, we can think about envy in these terms: the presence of something good is experienced (in part) as the absence of something bad – and as a corollary, the presence of something bad is experienced as the absence of something good. Therefore, there is a case for suggesting that soft innovation in part appeals to these drivers of behaviour, emotions which are as close to us and problematic as siblings.

---

26. Often as a 'weapon' to prevent action by others, and force changes in ownership www.nytimes.com/2012/10/08/technology/patent-wars-among-tech-giants-can-stifle-competition.html?pagewanted=all&_r=0.

PERSONALISATION

...questions, comments, conjectures....from the point of view of our propositions...

Our 9th point of view on innovation – personalisation – is a form of soft innovation where the of users of the service provide the innovative input in the way that products and services get combined, or distributed. In some essential way, they participate in the supply of goods and services to themselves. This is a curious phenomena – as if suddenly we all started to grow our own food, not for one other, but for ourselves. There is something highly individualised about it. An extension of it will be the 3D printing of your own body parts. Such innovation is based on use of intimate technologies.

The AppStore is an example of this, as is much of iWorld. I have an iPad and iPhone – and even though I know that millions of other people also are having this experience, I feel as though it has been customised to my needs and my taste. Such is the intimacy of my relationship with the stripped down aesthetic of its aluminum body, intuitive response to my touch and stroke, and retina display that I find myself believing that it exists for me. Without me realizing, I have an extension of my desires; a kind of avatar that helps me to work, love, know, plot... And – I conjecture – every other user and owner has this experience, feeling it to be unique to them while knowing it is (near universal) common place.

So, as the marketeers hanker after, frictionless distribution is achieved, with me doing the work. In the ideas of *iDemocracy*[27] and other forms of hyper-personalisation, I am become my own niche, in which I am immersed. Risk and welfare are socialized into the self.

In 2008, the UK Government introduced a policy to 'personalise' Adult Social Care investment. The policy vision behind this is to allow care recipients to become their own commissioners. I was recently in conversation with a Director of Adult Social Care who was describing a young man who had been in and out of mental institutions for the past 10 years. Under the personalisation of his own care, he was using the public funds to which he was entitled to pay for judo lessons. This had kept him out of hospital for the past 18 months. 'He's a better commissioner of services to meet his needs than I am,' said the Director.

As a model it depends on engagement of the service user in their own diagnosis and procurement of services; it may involve brokerage by intermediaries; and from a strategic point of view it requires the development of a mixed economy of high quality provision. It has also involved the development of forms of social purchasing (like Southwark Circle) as crowd sourced solutions for commissioning care. Care outcomes improve through my own intimate involvement in my care.

The UK Government White Paper on Open Public Services (2011) discusses extending these principles to every public service (except security services, the military and judiciary).

27. Douglas Carswell (2011).

CREATIVE DESTRUCTION

...questions, comments, conjectures....from the point of view of our propositions...

First articulated in 19th century by Karl Marx (as an inevitable consequence of capitalist wealth accumulation), since the 1950s creative destruction has been mainly associated with the ideas of Joseph Schumpeter. The connection between creativity and destruction seems (almost) 'natural' – and certainly seems to be a feature of regeneration cycles in biological systems. Some conjecture that the origins of this idea, lie in the qualities of the Hindu god, Shiva, the *Lord of the Dance*; in which creativity and destruction consort with one another (in itself an intimate image of tension and co-ordination). One might argue, our current economic crisis has made some of the implications of 'creative destruction' and 'destructive enterprises' too much to bear – as if we were saying, 'when I meant be creative, I didn't mean be this destructive...'

These theories apply profoundly to the current (2010 - 2013) European political and economic crisis – where there is a fear that 'disloyalty' to the euro would engender destruction on a beyond-creative scale. Whereas one could argue that the idea around which there needs to be some creative destruction is that of 'credit and debt' and economies buoyed up by debt. My choices about the quality of life in Greece extend beyond holidays and yoghurt. My wallet and their belly are linked.

Creative destruction and envy can also be linked – in so far as the absence of something good is experienced as the presence of something bad (a driver of consumer capitalism as engrained in our intimate selves, as stocking up on fat and sugar whenever we can as our Neanderthal natures walk through downtown).

There is a link with the socialization of welfare – and the dismantling of the post 2nd world war consensus in the West that (somehow) 'we-would-look-out-for-one-another'. It seems as if – within our current drivers around taxation (in the past 30 years relatively low taxes has moved from being an assumption on the part of part the political class, to be a driver of democracy) – this is in the process of being creatively destroyed.

Intimate experiences of creative destruction take the form of a little 'death', and as a change of identity, a breakthrough that can veer off into a breakdown. A new experience can crack up the carapace of an established way of seeing things, and following a period of re-patterning, re-form. In such a way, I am reformed. I can rise up against my own establishment, and initiate my own reformation; or collapse.

BIOMIMICRY

...questions, comments, conjectures....from the point of view of our propositions...

The core idea in biomimicry is that Nature, 'imaginative' (or at least varied & resourceful) by necessity, has already solved many of the problems we are grappling with. The 'technology' of biomimicry draws (on the one hand), on a detailed understanding of how particular organisms and biological systems have solved problems of sustained adaptation to their context (as that context has changed). On the other hand, it is also deeply informed by an understanding of the dynamics of biological systems and ecosystems. One could argue that it is a *micro and meta* theory of innovation – in the attention to design detail, and the whole system grasp of the relationship between small detail and context.

As such, feedback loops, attending to detail (often through the role of the biologist-by-design), and sensitivity to context, are core features of biomimicry. The view of hierarchy is also different in a biomimic world view – in so far as systems are build from hierarchies of interlinked sub systems which have the capacity to aggregate and disaggregate without loss of integrity to the system as a whole.

These are inter-subjective relationships. The technology of biomimicry – and its aesthetic – is on the small scale, the close at hand: it is a practical working through and application of Blake's 'world in a grain of sand'.

There are many many instances of the design-dynamic of biomimicry in all fields – ranging from the behaviour of slime mould modelling how transport distribution could work; or the heat-seeking properties of a desert snake leading to the design of the side-winder missile system. To name but one systemic illustration, there is also striking evidence of how root systems in forests distribute information about changes in concentrations or availability of nutrients.

But it also is the shaping force behind macro-economic re-modelling. The Helen McArthur Foundation has recently commissioned work to help develop the concept of the circular economy —an industrial system that is restorative by design, proposing that our systems should work like organisms, processing nutrients that can be fed back into the life-cycle. This is a direct parallel with the role of groups in helping their participants to metabolise their emotions through intimate connection with one another.

These features of biomimicry – the emphasis on closed systems, on feedback loops, on attention to details, on the very close relationship between the very small and the very big – the specific and the systemic – these are all aspects of our emerging concept of intimacy in relation to innovation. So, I am to some degree my own biomimic when I take account of the role of intimacy in innovation.

CONSCIOUS INNOVATION

...questions, comments, conjectures....from the point of view of our propositions...

Mandalah (www.mandalah.com) is a global innovation company head quartered in Sao Paulo, Brazil. They are devoted to working with detail, in their innovation practice, since they know that every gesture counts.

They co-create approaches to innovation with their clients, which draw on multi disciplinary and deliberately international points-of-view.

They have fun with complexity. Since they have found that the challenge of sustainability relies – in part – on engagement with complexity being maintained. And I am more likely to remain involved if I am having fun. I can tolerate my relationship to complexity for longer.

They customize the execution of each assignment as if they were inventing a stimulating framework from fresh, based around complementary ideas. They curate experience as much as they plan it.

They draw on systems thinking, complexity theory, integral theory, design thinking, and biomimicry – but these ideas have been used to *inform* the design of a series of unusual working methods.

These working methods include, for example:

- Learning journeys – real life immersions and stimulating trips around the world to absorb the specific fine grain of a context.

- Dialogue - with sensitivity, used lightly, subtly and compassionately, dialogues make a difference. They make the world more plural, and better.

- Meeting one another in unusual settings – working together on a beach, going for walks rather than staying in the board room.

There is a tacit acceptance in their approach that sees the value in intimacy as the basic condition of innovation. Indeed, many of the ideas in this book came into sharp focus working with Mandalah on a project on mobility in *mega-cities*, where we worked together for 9 months to innovate around this theme.

INNOVATING THROUGH SHARED EXPERIENCE

I tend to learn through shared experience – even if the other with whom I share is imagined by me. Extending this idea, I change my mind through shared experience. Extending this idea further, I innovate through shared experience.

Some of the real 'others' and imaginary 'others' are outside of me – some of the real and imagined others are parts of myself. There is an idea from psychoanalysis that part of what therapy does is introduce different parts of myself to each other....and through this special kind of social process, I develop my capacity to relate. And this process of therapy – and the capacity for relating in me that it can help develop – is a mix of insight and interaction, of interpretation and regulation (to use a therapeutic way of talking.)

Innovation involves something about 'insight' – about 'ah-ha' moments where something is placed in different relation to something else – much as a metaphor might work. Familiar creative processes like 'lateral thinking' or 'brain storming' are ways of creating the conditions for more 'ah-ha' and less 'yawn-yawn'.

Systems are made up of relationships; relationship is the context for insight, but there is more to it than that. Relationships are regulated through feedback – moment by moment experience of which involves 'attunement' – attunement to the qualities of relatedness in connection with

- Context
- Customers
- Competitors
- Colleagues

….and oneself. So, I am visualising an innovative, dynamic system in which there is both capacity for insight and capacity for regulation. This is part of what I mean by intimate innovation. And we might meaningfully link 'regulation' and 'governance' as concepts with different overtones – but deriving their meaning in innovation from a core:

- governance concerning the extent to which you have internalised your purpose; and

- regulation concerning the capacity to internalise meaning, such as purpose.

What are the qualities of shared experience where one is aware of the balance of insight and regulation? In the experiencing of shared experience, there is a stream of moments; this can feel like the way that people speak of quantum reality – where everything is happening all at once.

Some of these moments have a special quality – they are moments of inflection – based on an action of bending inwards – where the action of regulation and insight are the same thing.

This involves attending to minute details – attending to the 'shaping' effect of narrative about 'what-is-going-on' – and....

....to what is too hard to contemplate directly...to hold in your gaze...you can see it out of the corner of your eye, at a glance. The movement of a glance into a gaze. (This is my attempt to create a 'strap line' for this experience!)

Where is it that this intimate innovation takes place? In me, in you – between us – in the relatedness which we 'make up'. You and I are part of this essential context.

In their book *Emotional Contagion*[28] (quoted by Malcolm Gladwell in the *Tipping Point* (2002 page 84) Elaine Hatfield, John Cacioppo, and Richard Rapson explore the metaphor of 'contagion' in relation to emotions. They argue that mimicry is one of the ways by which we 'infect' one another with our emotions. Emotion is contagious – through facial expressions, gesture, body language. And as Malcolm Gladwell argues in *Blink* (his 2005 sequel to the *Tipping Point*), we are not aware that these micro, milli, nano experiences are taking place, and having a shaping effect on our emotional life. This 'shaping effect' is the 'shaping influence of attention' that we are connecting to regulation and attunement.

---

28. Emotional Contagion Elaine Hatfield, John Cacioppo, Richard Rapson (Cambridge: Cambridge University Press1994)

A few pages further on in the *Tipping Point* (2002) Malcolm Gladwell writes:

'We normally think of the expressions on our face as the reflection of an inner state. I feel happy so I smile, I feel sad so I frown. Emotion goes inside out. Emotional contagion, though, suggests that the opposite is also true. If I can make you smile, I can make you happy. If I can make you frown, I can make you sad. Emotion in this sense goes outside-in' (page 85)

This is the territory we are on; intimate innovation goes both inside-out and outside-in.

This is the quality of the Mobius strip we mentioned earlier.

Gladwell goes on to explore 'the power of context', and 'the fact that context is everything' when understanding the 'fit' between an epidemic and its 'spread' through a series of tipping points.

In his discussion of 'transactive memory' (pages 188 & 189), he describes how part of what intimacy means is 'sharing memories' with one's partner – not only in the sense of reminiscing, but in the sense that *part of my capacity to remember* is directly linked to my partner. In our terms, my partner is part of my capacity to innovate.

Gladwell goes on to describe: *'that is the paradox of the epidemic: that in order to create one contagious movement, you often have to create many small movements first.'* (page 192)

In the intimate view of innovation, I reach my own 'tipping point' – I become part of the context that is everything, experiencing many of the phenomenon that Gladwell describes from the outside, including:

- the power of weak ties;
- the fact that little changes have big effects;
- that non verbal is as (if not more) important than verbal communication; and
- that persuasion is established through the subtle, the hidden, the unspoken.

Intimate innovation is a way of surfacing the subtle but hidden; voicing something experienced but – typically - unspoken.

IN THE HERE & NOW

As I mentioned at the outset, the late Daniel Stern's ideas have been one of the inspirations behind this book. In this section, I want to especially explore some of his ideas[29] – on 'inter-subjectivity'. And we will connect these with our other ideas to develop a picture of the here-and-now actuality of innovating (when understood in the way that we are understanding it).

---

29. In doing this, I am drawing on material in *The Present Moment* (2004) and *Forms of Vitality* (2010). I am using his ideas as a jumping off point for my own – so they may well be connected in ways that do not reflect meanings that he intended by them. As such they are not an interpretation so much as a series of associations.

Stern introduces the topic of inter-subjectivity – as the inter-penetration of minds – by scoping the 'problem of now':

'The basic assumption is that change is based on lived experience. In and of itself, verbally understanding, explaining or narrating something is not sufficient to bring about change. There must also be an actual experience; a subjectively lived happening. An event must be lived, with feelings and actions taking place in real time, in the real world, with real people in a moment of presentness.' (page xiii Preface to The Present Moment)

This may risk labouring the point ….but pause and let these words register …

- change in based on lived experience….
- in and of itself, verbally understanding, explaining or narrating something is not sufficient to bring about change….
- there must be an actual experience….
- a subjectively lived happening…
- an event must be *lived*, with actions and feelings taking place in real time…
- with real people in a moment of presentness…

This is a commentary on the idea of 'changing my mind through a shared experience.' This seems to me to get under the skin of the notion that 'innovation is all about people' – it is only ever taking place between people; or without whatever is taking place between people, there won't be innovation.

There might be insight; but it won't stick. And it implies something also about the regulation of insight – not the control of it, but its mutual regulation, in its co-formation – it is a micro-interaction, a swarming of inter-subjective experience. Stern discusses examples of the lived experience he has in mind:

'Two simple examples of such lived experience are: looking at someone in the eyes who is looking at you and taking a deep breath while talking to someone. Both of these are actions with a feeling'. (page viii Preface to *The Present Moment*)

But we all know that experience is not this discrete – these examples are two shots from the movie of a few minutes of time spent together in shared experience. I struggle to find the image which captures this quality of amplified inter- subjective experience. There is:

- something 'quantum' about it – in so far as lived experiences are like protons or electrons, making up everything, yet invisible; they are not simply what matters – they are the *matter* – and our perception of them is often framed as an inquiry into 'what's the matter?'

- something animal about it – in so far as fish shoal, or birds flock – each individual acting as if there a nervous system to the collective (as if, relative to the observer, the flock has a 'mind-of-its-own');

- something fertile and random – like the sense of seed-fullness one gets in seeing the floating cloud of pollen, hum of insects and dust in sunlight; and

- something 'teeming', emergent, self-regulating.

Stern pushes his thinking about the lived experiences that are prior to their re-shaping in words[30] in stressing the significance of 'presentness':

'The idea of presentness is key. The present moment that I [Stern] am after is the moment of subjective experience as it is occurring – not as it is later reshaped by words. The present moment is the process unit for the experiences that will most interest us. A first step towards understanding experience is to explore and understand the present moment.' (Again from Preface to The Present Moment.)

Stern's interest is in exploring the connections between 'now' and therapeutic experience and processes; I have a different focus, although one could see therapy as a particular manifestation of intimate innovation. But much of what Stern explores in relation to therapy illuminates the process of intimate innovation.

He puts forward the idea of the present moment to deal with the 'problem of now', the fact that we are relatively ignorant of *now*. Even though this is the only place where we experience anything – this is where we directly live our lives – we have a great tendency to understand it at several removes (like 'in retrospect', 'in the past',

---

30. In writing this, I am struck by how much what I am re-shaping in words risks falling short of being a present moment between you and I.

even – in ways which relate especially (trickily) to innovation – 'in the future[31]'). Stern poses these questions:

'When is now? What is now? Does now exist and, if so, how long is it? How is now structured? What does it do? How is it related to consciousness, to the past? How does it lead to meanings? Why does it occupy such a special place in psychotherapy? And, related to these questions, how is now experienced when it is co-created and shared with someone? Finally, what role does now play in change?' (from Chapter One *The Present Moment*)

'Now' plays a no less significant role in innovation – it is the 'eureka' moment, the 'ah-ha!' of seeing something for what seems to be the first time. Some of this sense of 'now' in innovation comes from:

- insight into needs and wants;

- attention to context;

- openness to fresh association;

- knowledge of 'the competition'; and

- sufficient curiosity in the detail of a particular 'case' or 'dilemma' or 'challenge'.

---

31. Just pause to consider how much of the discourse of leadership is about predicting 'the future', about 'vision, about 'what will happen' – how inevitable a particular outcome will be. Yet the future is intrinsically unpredictable; therefore to predict is to repress possibility.

DYNAMICS RATHER THAN METHOD

I have considered how intimate innovation adds to - and relates with - other views of innovation. So much discussion about innovation talks about 'methods' and 'techniques'. And so much of the latent potential for innovation lies in the use of and development of technology. But I am visualising a form of innovation which uses soft technology, not hard.

But it is a soft technology that can be hard on you; in innovating like this, you pay with parts of yourself. Things change in you - and for you. Then they can be lastingly different.

Our theme and propositions are about dynamics, rather than technique; about relationship and relating as the creation-of-conditions-as-method, rather than method as a kind of tool or template. If you were running for office on an intimate innovation ticket, your campaign slogan could be, 'it's the relationship, stupid' (if you could find an appropriate way of saying 'stupid' without jeopardising intimacy).

It is common to hear people say 'everything is connected' – I am proposing an awareness and appreciation of this that is 'micro' in the experiencing of it, but has a 'macro' impact – like a benign contagion: the blooming of coral, or the viral spread of bacteria, or the way colour behaves in water.

Brain storming and techniques like that which proliferate possibilities, try to open up the processes of working on how to change the minds in a group (even, often, change the mind-of-the-group) without substituting one old group think with another, new group think. What might be the outcome of brainstorming ways to be intimate?

You and I make the rules for our particular intimacy – we are ethical, yet non-compliant. You are a challenge to me – but one I am prepared to accept. I am a challenge to you – but one you are prepared to accept. So the argot of challenge is reciprocal – it is two way; that, I am proposing, is the nature of the intimate challenge. You are watching me; I am watching you. We are sensing one another.

It is part of my contention that what technology[32] does is allow the dynamism to be contained – to be heightened – and this, in turn, can help to draw attention to the experience of it. Indeed, it might be that *all that technology does is allow the dynamism to be contained*; to be heightened – to draw attention to the experience of it; and, therefore, part of the value of the technology is aesthetic. And in this sense, there is something intrinsically intimate in the uses of technology – in the same way that Christopher Bollas[33] speaks of the 'vitality of objects', we are contending that there is something vital (and intimate) about technology.

It is a soft technology which helps us to be ethical, yet non compliant, through which you and I make and break our own rules; we become the cultural conditions under which innovation takes place. Soft technology that allows the dynamism of our inter-connectedness to be contained – and in so doing, it is heightened. It gains meaning.

---

32. By technology I mean 'a way of working', or 'a method or a device for helping us to do the work' whatever the work might be.

33. For example see: www.lrb.co.uk/v32/n05/jonathan-lear/sharing-secrets.

IMPLICATIONS OF INTIMACY IN INNOVATION

What are the implications of this intimate stance? what are likely to be some of the characteristics of new experiences - of myself, of you, or of us (from either point of view)?

new experiences of myself...
new experiences of yourself...
new experiences of myself _of_ yourself...
new experiences of yourself _of_ myself...
new experiences of the other, of my other, of your other...
of each other...

....and so on and so on....

Perhaps this is one of the central implications - the poly dimensional, multi layered, inner worlds and outer worlds taking each other into one another's space....not so much the world in a grain of sand, as a world of grains, of sands....deserts and beaches.

The innovative encounter 'takes on' the qualities of another (inner) world. And I encourage you to consider the ambiguity, the suggestiveness of 'taking on' as an idiom. How we use the term – and what we mean, and suggest by it – including:

- how we have a 'take' on something – a point of view, a position, an angle, an approach – and how this 'take' is propositional ('I put it to you that this is so and so....');

- how, when we 'take on', we are adopting – as in 'she took on the role'…'he took on the expression, the guise…'; and,

- how we 'take on' when we confront, we challenge, we act to re-balance – even to seek justice or enact vengeance – as in 'she took on the opposition…'.

Innovative encounters 'take on' the qualities of another inner world – having a take, adopting, confronting – an act of adoption which is also a confrontation.

In this intimately innovative and dynamic space, things are likely to be…

…friendly…informal….warm; yet….

…with latent challenge and potential for confrontation….; but…

…associative - both social and somewhere that meanings emerge, through connections being made…; also…

…somewhere, where my intimacy is my responsibility…; and…

…your intimacy is your responsibility… ; not withstanding…

…I am accountable for my own intimacy…

…you are accountable for your own intimacy…

…we are responsible for each other's intimate encounters…

...we are accountable to each other for each others' intimate encounters...

This space has something round it that resembles a boundary, but it is not a line, not a hard boundary ... it is more a zone into which something dissolves...like colour mixing, as we mentioned earlier...or the border between two countries that is unpatrolled, where there is a no-man's - land.

...Where will it end?
...What will it take to recover?
...Where things end is a sign of intimacy to me - I have reached a limit, my limit.

...Where I end and you begin, where I begin and you end is a - maybe *the* - place of intimacy for me....

...*and...what's more*...this implies that in order to innovate, I need to engage with *that which is*...

...pertaining to my inmost nature, essential...
...intrinsic...
...proceeding from, concerning my in most thoughts and feelings...
...close to a sensation of union...
...thoroughly mixed...
...mixed-up...

and there is likely to be an experience of something extensive....at times unbounded...that is...

...interpenetrative
...consensual
...tender
...aggressive
...hungry
...satisfied
...open to betrayal, for it is only if you know me that I can be betrayed by you...and if you did not know me, we could not be intimate....Given this, I suppose I can imagine being unconditionally innovative, have that fantasy to fall back on - but under what conditions?

But I am most interested in conditional intimacy – not some dream state, not some euphoric sense of loss, but something where lastingingly new *experiencing* can take place and new ideas are had; where it is possible to keep-on-changing-one's mind. Let's see what more we can find out about that.

THE CONDITIONS FOR INTIMATE INNOVATION

Theorists & practitioners of innovation often talk about 'conditions' – in that 'are the conditions right?' or 'have you created the right conditions?'. And the Google alerts I have been running which searched on 'intimate innovation' generated results which talk about:

- innovation taking place in intimate conference settings; and

- intimate conversations taking place which are more likely to lead to innovation.

So, we see a picture in which 'hygiene' conditions need to be satisfied, and if they are 'intimate' hygiene conditions, all well and good. Then there are a series of what one might call 'cultural conditions[34]'. Under this view the conditions for innovation depend on factors like appetite for risk, lack of knee jerk responses that blame others.

Then there are a series of 'social' conditions – these being part of the orthodoxy of our times – and many of these social conditions are based on social networking models (NESTA for example speak of

---

34. Spookily as I write this I have had an e mail from one such – the Centre for Public Innovation www.publicinnovation.org.uk. A guide to their *Insights into Innovation from the past 10 years* in which there is an image of a sun lounger with umbrella, with the headline 'Have you created the right conditions?'

'extreme collaboration[35]' as a key to the future of innovation). It is interesting at the moment how much the 'collaborative' assumptions about social conditions for innovation have prevailed – I guess it is partly a by-product of what is intrinsic to such conditions: they are bound to make many many connections. But within this special instance of the social conditions – there is a set of transactional or inter-active conditions, which can also tip over into their opposite, and stifle innovation. Under such conditions, however, intimacy is contained; we can be close, but not too close, attending to our own intra-subjectivity and our mutual inter-subjectivity.

A recent piece in the New York Times described the *Rise of the New Group Think*[36]. In it, the author of *Quiet* (2012), Sarah Cain argues against the hegemony of brainstorming in favour of informal associations between all kinds of people getting on for most of the time with their own thing. She writes:

'*Solitude has long been associated with creativity and transcendence. "Without great solitude, no serious work is possible," Picasso said.*

'*Culturally, we're often so dazzled by charisma that we overlook the quiet part of the creative process. Consider Apple. In the wake of Steve Jobs's death, we've seen a profusion of myths about the company's success. Most focus on Mr. Jobs's supernatural magnetism*

---

35. See www.intimate-innovation.co.uk for some ideas about 'degrees' of joint working, which are in effect degrees of openness to being changed by an-other which work both ways.

36. www.nytimes.com/2012/01/15/opinion/sunday/the-rise-of-the-new-groupthink.html.

and tend to ignore the other crucial figure in Apple's creation: a kindly, introverted engineering wizard, Steve Wozniak, who toiled alone on a beloved invention, the personal computer'.

The article sparked a series of responses from readers, in which – from varying points of view – they wanted to 'add back in' the intimate (through co-intelligence, through stressing the value of peer to peer learning, through the rule-generating by-products of working closely together).

It strikes me as I write this that all I may have been doing here is re-describing to you, Maslow's hierarchy of needs.

But I am also suggesting something else - that you are 'the conditions'; that I am 'the conditions'. In other words, when innovation is taking place it is only ever taking place within us and between us, in relation to one another. Innovation is dependent on the conditions in which and under which we relate – to ourselves and to one another. It is a by product of the conditions in the liminal[37] space between us.
So, we might say, that we are the conditions under which innovation can either take place or not – it doesn't happen 'out there', somewhere; it happens 'in here', somewhere. You know the idiom – 'she is in her element – (used to describe a state of affairs that is true to one's nature, primordial, basic, from which the rest is composed.) The term also suggests 'a hint'; an element is something crucial, but small – an inflexion which changes what is meant.

Using this language, we are our own element; intimacy is elemental to innovation.

---

37. Liminal meaning 'on a threshold', which is also a boundary – I suppose a way out as much as a way in, a preventer as much as a facilitator. It also carries with it the risk of 'being marginal' – of being irrelevant, small, easily over-looked, yet aware (from the margins) of something not visible in the main stream of the text, the mainstream of the group, the organisation, the market.

CHAPTER 3

CHAPTER THREE: HOW DOES INTIMATE INNOVATION WORK?

I have already discussed some of the dynamic aspects of our theme, and how they inter-play with one another - having in mind the dynamics of dance and gesture and mark-making, rather than the dynamics of - say - hydraulics, or mechanics. So we have been exploring ways in which innovation is intimate to the extent that it is:

- informal and hyper - social, but

- able to accommodate the two-of-us - as a property of a 'system';

- how it can resemble a 'quiet storm' - involving all of me - well at least more of me than I am used to - than I am prepared for; I am not prepared for intimate innovation - something in me gets prepared by the experience.

Further to this, in this chapter, we consider:

- if there isn't a method - one would be suspicious of someone who claimed to be methodically intimate - how do you 'do' it? Or if it is not a technique, then 'doing it' is mis leading.

- So we need to think about how to *create the conditions for intimate innovation*. Perhaps – then - we can, think in terms of how we manage the conditions....

OUR OWN EXPERIENCE OF INNOVATION

But what do we know from our shared experience about intimacy - what is 'intimated' by this question? What is hinted at? What is outlined? What is sensed if not perceived concretely..?

In some sense or another, we have an intimate relation with ourselves – we must be more or less close to ourselves. When we speak of a sense of self – we speak of what we know to be the case about ourselves; some of which we take for granted, some of which we assume; some of which we are driven by. But although it is not usually put like this, we are intimately involved with ourselves in all kinds of ways. And the idioms – 'she is self-absorbed', 'he is self-obsessed' – suggest that one can be intimate with oneself to a healthy degree, but beyond a certain point it becomes a malaise.

Innovation is about the origination of new relationships – between people, between ideas. But the point is that it is the moment of origination that matters; and that a process of innovation – the management of a process – will be to do with the sequence of moments. At the time, we will never know what is going to happen next, unless we pretend that robbing the future of its capacity to surprise is part of management[38].

And in intimacy, something actual is going on – but not necessarily something real. There can be actual intimacy, which is not real

---

38. Or part of the role that we assign to management, in scape-goating our leaders.

intimacy. Where we are really captured – or is it actually captured (?) – by our imaginations. As I said earlier... involving all of me - well at least more of me than I am used to - than I am prepared for...I am not prepared for intimate innovation - something in me gets prepared by the experience.

Captured, in our imaginations; captured by our imaginations. What is going on? Surely, I have to be an expert in my own intimacy; and you have to be an expert in your own intimacy. If we do not accept this as a basis of consent and of free association, where is it that I can be intimate from?

I am picturing innovation as the antithesis of tyranny – and by tyranny I mean a stance under which someone insists that they are loved[39].

'You will love me – no matter what', says the tyrant. Dictators require absolute obedience and absolute love – the scope for dissent or difference being narrowed down to terror. Under such a political (and mental) regime, the capacity to notice, respond to, and make use of difference is collapsed.

I would argue, you cannot have a new idea when subjected to tyranny. And when leaders and managers – or any of us – speak of '*driving* through a change' (or some personal, unflinching insistence), they are moving to act and speak tyrannically.

---

39. As discussed by Winnicott in '*Some Thoughts on the Meaning of the Word Democracy*' (1962) as quoted by Adam Phillips in 'Equals' Faber (2002).

I am not here to consume me, or consume you...that would be a perverse expression of intimacy between people. Yet if you resist the impulse to reify choice, you preserve the capacity for consent and you allow for – at least the idea of – intimate innovation...so maybe our ideas of intimacy in relation to innovation explain the balancing act between the risks of tyrannising people as consumers and allowing for the conditions under which we are free to change our minds[40].

SPACE AND TIME

...and maybe the only choice I can really exercise is over how close I am to you, how close I let you be: where the 'you' could be you, your service, your product, your cause.

We share this experience in a space where I can change, or at least where there is a possibility of me moving in ways which are new to me, and being moved in ways which are new to me.

The same could be, can be true for you – we could move into a space where both you and I are both open to change.

In *The Present Moment* (page 7), Daniel Stern discusses, the Greek concept of subjective time, *kairos*. He discusses how one of the origins of the word comes from the shepherds watching the stars. As the night progresses and the stars turn in the sky, they appear to

---

40. See www.intimate-innovation.co.uk where we discuss products and services in which we are intimately involved; on the one hand they bind us through dependency, and on the other hand seem to set us free.

rise and then fall against the horizon. The moment when a star has reached its apogee and appears to change direction from ascending to descending, is its *kairos*. It is:

'... the passing moment in which something happens as the time unfolds. It is the coming into being of a new state of things and it happens in a moment of awareness. It has its own boundaries and escapes or transcends the passage of linear time. Yet it also contains a past. It is a subjective parenthesis set off from chronos'.

'*Kairos is a moment of opportunity, when events demand action or are propitious for action. Events have come together in this moment and the meeting enters awareness such that action must be taken, now, to alter ones destiny – be it for the next minute or a lifetime. If no action is taken, one's destiny will be changed anyway, but differently, because one did not act. It is a small window of becoming and opportunity'.*

So what might this *mean* for innovation?

Well I wonder? What occurs to you? Perhaps we could see innovation as…

- close at hand, and in some ways small scale;

- a personal experience that this amplified and experienced with greater complexity when shared;

- going on, taking place inside…and between…;

- something which somehow, we both make happen;

- as space in which gestures count ….and ….it is a space…;

- …in which we can change…we can have new experiences…;

- a space in which it is possible to have new experience with yourself and with others;

- where change takes place concurrently…they take place now, but lastingly so…where 'events' seem to have a different connection to time than they usually do…they can stretch from the past into the future…they cast a shadow full of light…they can seem like a perpetual moment…;

- where I can be rich in memory, where the richness of my memory is provoked, if not caused – I lapse into reverie…where I can be rich in fantasy….

Could these ideas become part of what we mean when we say, 'let's innovate'?

WHEN SOMETHING IS TOUCHING

There is so much talk in management, and leadership, and social policy and politics about – 'taking responsibility' and 'empowerment' and 'bottom up decision making' and 'engagement'. And in essence all of these are impulses to 'move power to the edge' – where the dynamics of intimacy are more likely to be at play.

There are so many instances of this principle… 'outliers' come from the edge; the 'scouts' come in from the edge, having been in contact with other tribes, other worlds, other systems…maybe there is a connection between 'edginess' and innovation. Think about a company like Diesel, for example – which is well known for sending its designers out, around the world, to find ideas for new products, new materials, a new aesthetic.

Maybe there is something special about 'design'…maybe it is in intimate relation that the possibility of the re-design of experience is possible – so something seems to link edge with intimacy with design…

And then there is the blurring, warping, bending, dissolving, breaching of boundaries that can happen…or the moving into a boundary zone where beginnings and endings are unclear, and the lack of clarity feels like an edge of some kind. When I say I am 'on edge', or 'feeling edgy', is this what is happening?

What is going on? Am I letting something in…letting someone in…. being let in…

Are we seeking to connect - deeply, lastingly – or is there a too-great-to-be-risked risk at play?

I attended a conference in Melbourne in June 2011, and after it had finished I went to the state art gallery, where there was a collection of Aboriginal Art – under one of the diptychs, was the phrase: 'your dream is your skin'.

Intimacy is to do with touch – with being touched – with touching…
with something 'being touching'…with being 'in touch'… somehow to
do with my skin, but going deeper…is anything deeper than my skin?

There maybe something in these themes which means that the
surface is as deep as it is shallow; and that 'being untouchable[41]'
makes innovation unlikely, if not impossible. If I am not open (to an
experience touching me) then I am less likely to change.

And there is some kind of escape, involved…yet some kind of escape
that is somehow real - yet not real escape *away* – it is an escape
into…an escape into me, with you…an escape into you, by me…
where I begin and end gets confused – beginnings and ends get
mixed up.

So what more might this *mean* for innovation? It seems to me that
innovation viewed in this way might primarily be about…

- relating and making connections between ideas, people, parts of the system … making connections where they did not exist, or only in imaginary form – in fantasy;

- heightened emotion and the deliberate heightening of emotion might create the conditions where innovation is more likely;

---

41. One can see some professions in this kind of light – indeed it is one of the unfortunate by products of a 'profession' that it makes itself more or less 'untouchable'; closed off from influence by the outside. In this sense, some forms of self-regulation are inimicable to innovation: they are not mutual.

- a space where identities are open to change – a kind of definition of innovation;

- a space where resistance is visible and open to being reduced – itself a pre-condition of change.

Both informal and hyper – social, but able to accommodate the two-of-us as a property of the 'innovative system'. We are moving away from – but not abandoning – the idea of collaboration as a primary source of innovation; there is such a thing as collaborative advantage. But perhaps there is a case for seeing the substantive collaborative advantage as an intimate collaboration.

Perhaps alongside the dominant metaphors of competitive advantage, we can risk thinking of 'intimate advantage'? After all, what does 'patient centred' mean if not this? What does 'putting the child at the centre of the care system', mean if not this? What does 'being close to the customer' mean, if not this?

You don't become the patient, become the child, become the customer; but without losing yourself, you do see and experience the world – of your services, your system etc – as they see and experience it. This seems to me to be pretty close to – if expressed in a way which is a bit dry, and abstracted – a form of intimacy.

There isn't a method – one would be suspicious of someone who claimed to be methodically intimate – so there is something 'informal' going on – which at the same time 'informs', provides an informing impulse – is an important kind of information. Can I claim that I am in-formation when I am intimate?

If I am 'in-formation' when I am intimate, then what does that say about 'information'? What would intimate information be like? What would be the data? What would be the data governance protocol....?

DISRUPTION AND BETRAYAL

You have an unexpected effect on me. Your being so close in the way that you are is a form of disturbance; although I also – ambivalent somewhere in the heart of me – feel it to be an opposite of neglect... as if when I am not intimate, I am involved in a form of self-neglect.

When intimate I am open to betrayal...I can only be betrayed[42] by someone close to me, someone who really knows something about me; yet if I do not get close to the experience, I am betraying myself.

...and in this close connection which brings knowledge, there is a risk – indeed a likelihood – of betrayal.

In the London Review of Books (LRB) in January 2012 Adam Phillips (in the text of a talk he would have given at St Paul's Cathedral if it had not been for the 'occupy' protests at that time) discusses betrayal and (amongst other things) innovation in a short piece called *Judas' Gift*. In it he discusses how Bob Dylan notoriously betrayed some of his fans in playing an electric (rather than acoustic) version of 'Like a

---

42. Just think about what it feels like to be 'let down' by a leader who you thought was both radical and ethical. I will never forgive Tony Blair.... and yet in order to protect myself from having an intimate relationship with any leader, I assume that they all tend to be unethical.

Rolling Stone' at Manchester Free Trade Hall and one of them called out 'Judas!' and Dylan said to his band, 'play louder'.

In his characteristic way, Adam Phillips[43] puts a series of conjectures 'out there':

'Here the betrayer is someone who wanted something to change; in retrospect we can see what sounded like a betrayal was innovation. Something was betrayed to make something else possible...'

He goes on to comment:

'...you can do lots of things with betrayal, but you can't undo it. It seems irredeemable. To betray is to create a situation that there is no going back from'.

If we think of betrayal as – in part – an act of innovation, this suggests that one of the fears of innovation is that there is no 'turning back'. Perhaps this is why 'classic' designs are seen as being of such value; or why innovations that 'hark back to an earlier, simpler' era are consistently popular. We have changed, but somehow stay the same. I have been betrayed, but I still trust. This seems to imply that it is only the virtue of forgiveness[44] that makes innovation possible.

Phillips continues....

---

43. I have been hugely influenced by Adam Phillips' writings – and applying some of his ideas to organisations and the world of organisations itself feels like a kind of betrayal. Although what is lost is hard for me to say.

44. And forgiveness corrupted is nostalgia.

'If betrayal is one of the ways, or the way, in which we change our lives, perhaps we should talk not only of the fear of being betrayed, but of the wish, the willingness to be betrayed, and to betray. We would be talking of betrayal as a transformational act; we might even talk of it as an object of desire and start noticing how we seek it. We might also start noticing all of the opportunities to betray and be betrayed that we have missed, risks that for various reasons we have avoided'.

I wonder if we can see innovation as an 'object of desire'? Policy makers and theorists certainly talk of it as-if-it-were. To some extent we did this in chapter two, *what is intimate innovation*. And if it is an object of desire, how does that make our relationship with it more complex, since complexity characterises our intimate desires? At the very least we are likely to certainly be ambivalent. And as an object of desire, an expression of our intimate self, and our relationship to that intimate self. So, perhaps, innovation and my sense of my own capacity in desiring the objects which I desire are linked.

As Adam Philips might well put it, 'I wonder what I am really doing when I innovate?'

CHANGING MY MIND

We have been conjecturing about some of the ways in which we are all intimate. But what might be the dynamics of how I change my mind?

- If innovation depends on me 'changing my mind', what is the dynamic of me changing my mind?

- If innovation depends on you 'changing your mind', what is the dynamic of you changing your mind?

There is a vast literature and related body of knowledge about this kind of thing; some of it based on neuro science, some on neuro-linguistic programming; some on theories of leadership; some on processes of change and innovation through which people are influenced.

I am suggesting that we under-interpret innovation by neglecting the mind-changing aspects of it; and – very importantly – therefore have unrealistic expectations of effectiveness. Much of the work we do to innovate is unlikely to gain traction or make a difference if we do not take account of one of the dynamic forces that helps us to change our minds and those of others. I am calling this dynamic force intimacy, since it is only in intimate relation to others, that one's mind is open to lasting change.

This intimate relation can be real or imagined – but my contention is that there is more scope for lasting change if the relation is real rather than imagined. Indeed if the intimacy is imagined – in fantasy, for example – it is more likely to lead to repetition. This repetition – especially if it is intimate to you - might feel fresh, charged, new – might indeed have many of the qualities of an innovative state, and the associated sense of 'having arrived', of having 'done something'. Yet, it risks being simply the same-old-stuff-feeling-new again.

Most intimacy in relation to innovation in organisations is, however, imagined. Leaders tend to have intimate relationships with imagined versions of their customers, and those that follow them; and those that follow, tend to have intimate relationships with imagined versions of those who lead them. We all rely on others to be real on our behalf –this maybe why fundamentally we organise at all.

Perhaps if we can get beyond the imagined to the real – get real and get intimate in our innovation – then we can reduce the drag, and increase the flow – convert more of the power of the wind into movement, as if one were sailing. All change is characterised by 'loss'. We may be willing to change, but we often act as if we can choose what we will lose. That would not be a loss; that would be choosing the form of pain one was willing to suffer – an elaborate way of remaining stuck whilst pretending to change. When I am 'at-a-loss', I might innovate.

FORMS OF VITALITY

Daniel Stern has written about dynamics in ways which help us. His field of interest is child development. In his work, *Forms of Vitality*, he discusses 'economy of effort' as a dynamic quality of dancers, and others whose modes of expression are physical. On page 6, Daniel Stern writes:

'Now zoom in to describe the dynamics of the very small events, lasting seconds, that make up the interpersonal, psychological moments of our lives: the force, speed, and flow of the gesture; the timing and stress of spoken phrase or even a word; the way one

breaks into a smile all the time course of decomposing the smile; the manner of shifting position in a chair; the time course of lifting the eyebrows when interested in a thought and the duration of their lift; the shift and flight of a gaze; and the rush or tumble thoughts. These are examples of the dynamic forms and dynamic experiences of everyday life. The scale is small, but that is where we live, and it makes up the matrix of experiencing other people and feeling their vitality'.

Pause. Re-read this list. Imagine each of these small events…imagine yourself doing them. Do them. Imagine being in the company of someone doing them. Move into the company of someone doing them. What's it like? What are the inflections of this way of looking at the day-to-day?

It is common to hear versions of the phrase, 'well if we carry on doing things the way we have always done them round here, then we'll get the same results'. And self help, self development books talk about developing 'new habits' – like crossing your arms the other way round, or taking a different route to work. All these impulses and points of view are designed to provide an experience of something new – to give you a feel for what it is like, in small ways, to innovate. *'Do it in small ways; do it in big.'* This seems to be the development principle – as if you can build up the capacity to innovate as if that capacity were muscle.

Yet that capacity to innovate is more like a brain, where capacity is dependent in the main on the variety and complexity of connectedness. The many many small inter-relationships remain many and small; but capacity derives from patterns of poly-connectedness.

Let's go back to Daniel Stern. His point of view suggests to me that maybe part of what we overlook when we try to observe, or discern, or capture innovative capacity is 'what-is-going-on'. What we miss is what we are actually doing, and if we could better apprehend what we are actually doing, then maybe our capacity for innovation would be enhanced, and could be applied to whatever purpose[45] we have in mind.

I am going to quote at length from the next sections of *Forms of Vitality*:

'The term dynamics has many meanings. Physics deals with the dynamics of objective forces that act to remove or equilibrate measurable systems. It is energy, power, and force in motion. Alternatively, it is change that is in process. It is the opposite of static'.

Again, I suggest you pause. We are exploring the idea that intimacy has a dynamic relationship to the capacity to innovate; to the extent that it is dynamic, it has some of the following properties….

- it deals with forces, and force/power;

- it equilibrates: it has to do with balancing, yet it also has to do with 'dis-equilibrating', with going off balance;

---

45. I see this as also a governance and self governance issue; since governance is the way that you internalise your purpose. As such, there can be intimate governance.

- it calibrates: there is some kind of measurement involved, some degree of intimacy, even if it is impossible to apply standards to it (although couples often do);

- it involves motion;

- it is change that is in process; and

- it is the opposite of static, and by implication, therefore, active rather than passive.

Daniel Stern further develops the idea of 'dynamics':

'In music, the term dynamics is usually restricted to changes in loudness (amplitude, is the product of force). The time course of the change is implied. In psychoanalysis, psychic forces and counter forces and their resultant experiences (psycho dynamics) act over developmental time to create a history of meanings. Thomson (1994) writes about, emotional dynamics, referring to the processes that create an emotion from mutually interacting inputs (forces) of arousal, cognitive appraisal, social contexts, etc. There are also the, dynamics, of our bodily movements in daily life in sports'.

He sums up this section of his book, with a discussion of the different ways in which you could describe dynamic forms of vitality:

'To understand dynamic forms of vitality more clearly, consider the following list of words

exploding	bursting	fleeting
swelling	disappearing	weakly
drawn out	powerful	tentative
forceful	pulsing	pushing
cresting	cooling	floating
rushing	languorous	easy
relaxing	effortful	halting
fluttering	gentle	tightly
tense	swinging	bounding
gliding	loosely	
holding still	accelerating	...and many more.
surging	fading	

Although these words are common enough, this list is curious. Most of the words are adverbs or adjectives. The items in it are not emotions. They are not motivational states. They are not pure perceptions. They are not sensations in the strict sense, as they have no modality. They are not direct cognitions in any usual sense. They are not acts, as they have no goals or date and no specific meanings. They fall in between all the cracks. They are the felt experience of force-in movement-with a temporal contour, and a sense of aliveness, of going somewhere. They do not belong to any particular content. There are more form than content. They concern the 'how', the manner, and the style, not the 'what' or 'why''. (from pages 6 & 7 in Forms of Vitality).

So what? What has this to do with our theme?

Daniel Stern seems to be saying that – to adapt some of his own words - regardless of the content (thoughts, actions, and emotions), this Gestalt of vitality has its own flow pattern (e.g. accelerating, exploding, and fading).

I think there is a parallel with some of our propositions. The dynamics of intimate innovation share many of the characteristics of Stern's notion of vitality. The qualities of intimate innovation are in the here and now of relating, in the small acts that make up our day to day relating. It constitutes a separate kind of experience – one 'hidden in plain view' – from the more conventional ways in which innovation is understood.

Innovation often relates to the wider considerations in organisational life of the 'what' (of strategy) and the 'why' (of purpose), but neglect of the 'how' of intimate innovation (amongst other things) jeopardises the fulfilment of purpose in the carrying out of strategy.

As Stern says, the scale is small; but that is where we live. I equally think that this is where we (start to) innovate. There is something we have over-looked in thinking about innovation – about this stream of almost constant ongoing changes that reignite and help maintain our sense of being alive. This is what innovation – in all its intimacy – is about.

How can we get this – more – into organisational life, and business? It is there – it-can't-not-be-there – but we tend to keep it 'hidden from view', on display below the surface.

COMPLIANCE AND CONSENT

There is a fundamental distinction in this application of the idea of the dynamics of intimacy to innovation. It is the distinction between consenting and complying. I can withhold of myself when I comply – I use myself and make myself available for your use when I consent.

The rhetoric around 'consultation', and 'buy in' in relation to innovation and change is about this. The UK Government's pre-occupation with 'behaviour' change and 'nudge' is essentially about the transformation of a social-contract-assumption about compliance and entitlement into a social contract based on a different balance of consent.

There is good evidence that this is in part about my identity; 'nudge' works if I am a member of a group who are also behaving as I am trying to behave eg. I am more likely to be able to give up smoking if I am in social groups with people who are also trying to give up smoking; I am more likely to be able to change my diet, or exercise habits if I am close to people either trying to do the same, or with whose behaviour I can identify. In other words, they are close enough to me; I am close enough to them. In our terms, we are intimate enough.

So, I can consent to comply if I am intimate. This is part of the basis of 'joining in' with anything – but, especially, it is intrinsic to joining in with anything new. In other words with innovation.

There is a fascinating application of this principle in the *Spirit Level* (2009 published by the Equality Trust) where fantasies of social mobility – a form of innovation - are discussed. It has been a mantra of social policy[46] in the UK and America for decades that inequity promotes meritocracy – if I (at the bottom of the social scale) can see that others have 'ascended' then I believe that I can. This generates a type of so-called social dynamism. But the vital detail – often hidden from view – is whether or not I identify with those 'other' people. Are they in some ways already like me; or am I sufficiently like them in some respects, to want to be more like them? And, therefore, strive.

In our terms, do I see myself as close enough to them to be able to fantasise that I could be intimate. The very phrase, quaint now, and from another era, 'they were intimates', captures this exactly.

The evidence in the *Spirit Level*, makes clear that this dynamic (in which I consent to comply – and therefore aspire) is only possible if the 'gap' between me and those I aspire to be intimate with is capable of being crossed in my fantasies.

Donald Winnicott has an interesting take on this topic, as he did on so much.

He did not think that the opposite of compliance was consent. He thought that the opposite of compliance was surprise[47]. Adam Phillips discusses how Winnicott (in his consultations with children) found

---

46. See www.wired.co.uk/magazine/archive/2012/06/ideas-bank/society-isnt-a-startup for a discussion of how 'sharing' can undermine 'caring'.
47. Discussed in passing in *Winnicott* (Fontana Modern Masters page 12 Kindle edition).

that the significant moments were ones in which the patient surprised herself. In fact the development of a capacity to be surprised by oneself could be said to be one of the aims of Winnicottian analysis.

This could be seen as a form of self-innovation.

Adam Phillips also makes the point that a surprise eludes the expectations made possible by a body of theory. It is a release from compliance – now and in the future, since surprise suggests that you don't know what is going to happen; whereas, the expectations of a body of theory are predictive. Depending on how you hold the theory, you risk only looking for what the theory illuminates or allows.

ADOPTION

A significant dimension of the dynamics of intimate innovation relates to adoption, as it near universally applied in innovation.

In discussions with Sarah Sutton, my fellow director at the *learning studio*, she has led my thinking about the term 'adoption'. She is a specialist in adoption in the childcare system. Her theorising about adoption imagines a child who has been relating - often in very disturbing ways - to a 'damaged object'. Neglect of the child has been intrinsic to this formative relating; and to some degree there is a dynamic in which the child plays their own part in this - where maintaining the familiarity of this particular form of neglect is part of their identity.

Part of what prevents the child 'being adopted' by the new parents (from the child's own world view, as experienced by the child in any event) is the child's attachment to the 'damaged object'; and the fear that if the child turned away from the damaged object, that damaged object (the existence of which, and the 'damaged' nature of which has been - may still persist in being - part of the child's world view) would die. This engenders a 'pitch' of anxiety which gets acted out.

In 1903, the first theorising about 'adopters' in relation to innovation was done by Gabriel Tarde. In Wikipedia, he is described as 'inventing innovation'. His model described a series of steps in the diffusion[48] of an innovation – which were made up of various degrees of acceptance and rejection. Innovators were in the vanguard, followed by early adopters and later adopters (and then – variously – 'laggards' or the 'rump' or the 'dies hards').

Some versions of the S curve model describe a 'chasm' – what follows is the template from Microsoft Visio. And much of the 'challenge' of successful innovation is perceived to be about 'bridging' the chasm, moving it to the right in the process (so that fewer and fewer people are beyond the chasm). The tactics discussed in management literature for tackling this are mainly drawn from military analogies – like the creation of a 'bridgehead', or a 'storm/tornado' of adoptees. But perhaps we need to re-imagine this as a process more akin to 'alignment'.

---

48. In itself a concept with which we are taking issue: we don't visualise innovation starting in one place, and being diffused, or spread. It is more like we create an innovation between us as if we were weaving it, or acting like a 3D printer, laying down nano layer by nano layer (like grapheme).

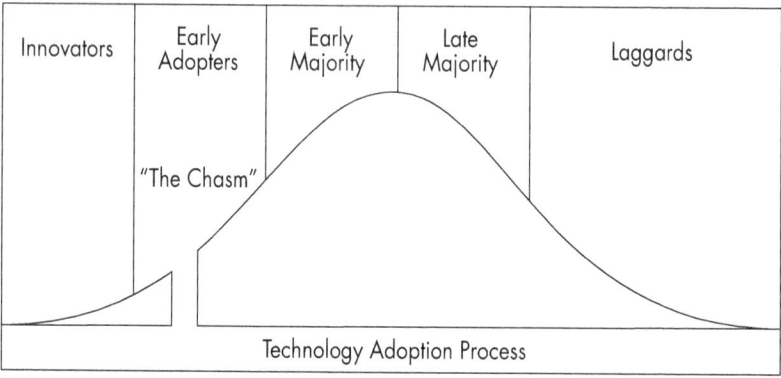

So we have a well established doctrine of the process of adoption in one sphere that might benefit from what is known in another sphere where the process of adoption is deeply understood and experienced.

As a result of what Sarah Sutton introduced to me, I have reflected on how evocative a parallel there is here (without in any way denigrating the pain of adoptive children, parents, and those who work with them) between the dynamics of child adoption and more general emotional responses to change, and innovation. When we 'adopt' innovations – with a relationship to our capacity to be intimate – we are in the business of 'alignment'; in some form or another, we reconceptualise the 'chasm' as a 'gap', which we can each reach across.

Models of innovation which stress adoption - where the innovation is vested in one and the necessity to adopt is in the many - are a species of either propaganda or tyranny.

Models of innovating which stress intimacy assume that inter-personal, inter-subjective encounters are the basis of lasting change - in which vulnerability is part of what is evident. I won't change my mind, unless I exchange with you - and part of the fundament exchange is to acknowledge my vulnerability - recognize our dependence - work through our mutual frustration.

In the childhood adoption instance, the 'damaged object' has to die - at least to the child as a dominant figure in its inner world. If the 'damaged object' will not die, then the child may have to 'murder' them. Or at the very least, the 'damaged object' and its memory (its memorialisation) has to be betrayed.

In terms of the life and death emotional stakes, this is what organisational change can feel like. And just as there is a narrative around adoption of children[49] that speaks of the virtues of a happy and stable home, there is equally an orthodoxy on the inevitable virtue of innovation. As if to be in a state of constant change were the paradigm.

And there is something about the process of adoption that is experienced as being 'taken in' – taken into a new 'happy home', and 'taken in' as duped (tricked into believing that this new place would be safe, tricked into denying the past). Many experiences of innovation feel like this – states in which I am 'taken over' rather than free to associate.

---

49. See the UK Government's recent (2012) adoption action plan for Michael Gove's lyrical policy statements on this.

Part of our proposition is that given this paradigm, attending to the very fabric of experience – in all its intimate, related detail – is central to making experiential sense of this, as well as a way of embodying innovation in how we relate to ourselves and one another.

Perhaps if we paid more attention to the intimate nature of innovation, between us, the chasm of adoption may itself change into something other than a gulf. Or at least the notion of chasm would lose some of its ominous character, and would become something more like a perforation, made up of 1000s of minute gaps – each one of which could be 'fired' across (like neural activity across synapses). There is something essentially synaptic rather than disruptive about this version of the process of innovation.

SOMETHING SOCIAL GOING ON

Conditions for intimate innovation are characterised by the absence of an agenda - or more specifically the transition to a new agenda where we are the agenda, and our relating is the business of the meeting; if we see agenda as a way of organising your emotions (and any risk of change to your identity) in advance of them being experienced. So, we are visualising meetings in which we meet, rather than settings in which I want to change you to be more like me.

...and yet it seems likely that intimate innovation could also be a new way of organising resistance, in so far as our being intimate reduces my inhibition....creates sufficient dis-inhibition for something new to happen; yet I need sufficient inhibition – in order to be able to see...

in order to be able to tell-what-is-happening....but sufficient dis-inhibition to join in.

There are many many ways in which the 'conditions' can be described – and I am drawn to suggest that it is important to try and keep 'multiple' or 'poly' perspectives in mind. As one might say in a quantum view of the world[50], all possible conditions all exist at the same time – it is only through collapsing the quantum reality into a local (could we say 'intimate' for local?) context, that any-one-thing-in-particular is real, in so far as it prevails. This quality of dis-orientating possibility is one of the main conditions.

The RSA is leading a project on the social brain[51]. This project has developed a series of working assumptions....and applies them to social engagement projects where there is a need to attend to change in behaviour. Although they do not describe behaviour change in terms of innovation, the principles make clear that there is an assumption of change – and of change taking place within and between individuals.

'Our experience[52] of working on habits, attention and decisions in practical contexts has given rise to the following working assumptions that underpin our approach:

---

50. This point was inspired by conversations with Philip Boxer. See his blog www.lacanticles.com/2012/09/the-quantum-metaphor/.
51. www.thersa.org/action-research-centre/social-brain/core-thematic-strands.
52. These principles were accessed from their www site on 13th November 2012.

We cannot change ourselves without changing each other
Most behaviour change does not occur at the level of the individual alone. Not only do we rely on other people to achieve the changes we seek to make, but such behaviours spread through social diffusion, and there is no way of knowing where our influence ends.

Complexity is more often the solution than the problem
To navigate a complicated world, we need complex minds. We need to work on having a 'relationship to our reactions', and when faced with multiple perspectives we should be able to both differentiate and integrate them.

It is better to be reasonable than rational
Clear thinking matters, but the touchstone of our thought should not be disembedded logic, but contextual sensitivity and concern for others.

Paying attention is good for you
We are what we attend to, and there are increasing demands on our attention. We need some resistance to the power of advertisements and the allure of technology. To avoid becoming slaves to the information and tools we use, we need to learn to pay closer attention to what is going on around us, within us and between us on a regular basis.

If we want new habits we should work with our habitats
We are creatures of habit, but unlike most creatures we have considerable power to shape our habitats for purposes beyond our basic needs. Behaviour change is not mainly about willpower, but

about using self-awareness to shape our environments so that our social and automatic brains align with our goals and values.

The brain is a stimulant
The brain is something we all have in common, and share an interest in. We use information about the brain as a socialising device to stimulate collective self-awareness. Through reflecting on the social and automatic nature of the brain, we learn how to change our behaviour for the better.

These working assumptions are a description of conditions – from one perspective – under which it would be possible to encourage intimate innovation. And they point in the direction of an understanding of society as a medium in which intimate innovation can take place – indeed the parallels (even if mainly metaphorical) in the dynamics of the social[53] and the brain are striking.

In the summer 2009 issue of the RSA Journal, Adam Zeman[54], discusses creativity in ways which reflect the working assumptions of the Social Brain Centre. He makes several points about conditions which foster creativity. He discusses the ways in which we are

---

53. David Eagleman in *Incognito the Secret Lives of the Brain* (Canongate 2011) discusses this – his idea of the brain being structured from a massive system of systems made up of specialist sub systems (a 'team of rivals' is how he puts it) is a profoundly social structure. It suggested to me that we could even think about a 'polis' of the brain, in which there was a kind of politics, a kind of self governance going on. What might be the equivalent of Plato's *Republic*, but of the brain? So, as well as being 'social', the brain is actually structured 'like a society'.

54. Part of the Insight/Cognition series; Adam Zeman is Professor of Cognition and Neurology at the Peninsula Medical School.

'*precisely* cultural animals'. We posses a series of 'capacities' (he calls them 'abilities') to help keep us social that are in the individual brain; many of these centre around the dynamics of 'mirror neurons' – and the ways in which patterning seems to develop – 'even, or perhaps, especially, at moments of improvisation'.

He concludes, '*Cultural creatures are driven by two opposing tendencies, both crucial to our way of life: we are inveterate rule makers and inveterate rule breakers*' (page 17 RSA Journal summer 2009).

Several ideas seem linked in this ….

- our social capacities – which are both inside us and outside us - are embodied in the fabric of society and the dynamics of our brains;

- their expression is in a set of rules which we need to transgress in particular ways (and these particular modes of rule making and rule breaking could be called 'a culture');

- the moment in which we unexpectedly apprehend a different pattern is a moment of innovation and potential change – and, as we have discussed, a moment of inflection; and

- a moment of improvisation in which the absence of rules to bind what might happen helps to facilitate the freedom to make something new together.

SURPRISE AND STRESS

There are countless examples in biological systems where shock is as much associated with fruiting as it is with dormancy. I am reminded of our earlier discussion of Adam Phillips of Donald Winnicott that the opposite of compliance may not be freedom, but surprise; and as Phillips himself says in *Side Effects* , '....*perhaps our preferred emotional depth charge is not loss or melancholy, but surprise*', suggesting that amongst other things risk, is a way of inducing surprise. And with surprise comes the possibility of innovation.

Surprise and stress seem to be closely related, in so far as the capacity to experience surprise is directly related to relative freedom from stress. It appears clear that one of the ways in which biological systems respond to stress in their environment, is to become dormant (or as we might say, entirely inhibited). When we become depressed or hyper-active, we are enacting something similar – shutting down our exposure to our own context, including what I can share with you, so that (amongst other things) there is less risk of surprise. As such, surprise is a species of shock – not so extreme as to lead you to freeze; but extreme enough to lead you to actually experience something 'other'.

In '*Working below the surface the emotional life of contemporary organisations*'[55] there is an essay called 'Leadership, followership, and facilitating the creative workplace' (by Anton Obholzer with Sarah Miller). In it, they write:

---

55. editors Clare Huffington, David Armstrong, William Holden, Linda Hoyle, and Jane Pooley. Karnac Books (published 2004) London.

'It is axiomatic that in instances where one's work provokes anxiety, an organisation's membership will be particularly caught up in enacting defensive processes, through personal valency (Bion 1961) and vulnerability' (page 40).

For 'anxiety' – in our terms – read 'stress'. They go onto to mention:

'Bion borrowed the concept of valency from physics, where it denotes the proclivity of an atom to combine with others. In his applied sense in the field of human unconscious group / institutional processes, he used it to mean "capacity for instantaneous, involuntary combinations of one individual with another sharing and acting on a basic assumption[56]". The connection between the individual and the institutional processes is thus via the valency factor of the individual's personality.'

This "capacity for instantaneous, involuntary combinations of one individual with another sharing and acting on a basic assumption" could be seen as a Bion-esque description of intimacy. But intimacy of a particular kind – one in which the acting on basic assumption tends to lead to a minimising of the likelihood of surprise. In other words, if I act out of my valency, I will tend to be intimate in the same way every time I combine with others. So, this movement has something of the quality of improvisation, but lacks something, too. If I am surprised in the same way every time, then this is merely a lively way of being stuck.

---

56. Bion meant something particular (and widely interpreted) by 'basic assumption'.

Although there is more to them than this, personality profiles – like the MBTI scores – in effect elaborate this point. When in the 'grip' (as they term it), each personality type will tend to have a default response, or valency. So, stress provokes default responses; and default responses have – in all probability – been developed in response to forms of stress (like hunger, trauma, neglect, lack of parental attunement etc).

So....we are discerning a pattern in which when subject to stress, I am likely to unconsciously depress (if not shut off) my capacity to either generate or experience surprise. And one of the ways in which this is manifest is that I will be intimate in the ways that I am used to being intimate – I will reduce the likelihood of surprise by making the future predictable.

In other words my valency will encourage dormancy, a condition under which innovation (as the surprise of the new) is least likely. And – I conjecture – that my capacity to break rules (by which culture can be kept vital) will also be reduced.

INTIMATE REGULATION

I would like to draw on some of the ideas of Allan Schore[57] who has researched and written extensively on the multi-disciplinary

---

57. UCLA David Geffen School of Medicine (see, for example, his plenary address to American Psychological Association Annual Convention (August 2009) 'The Paradigm Shift: the Right Brain and the Relational Unconscious'). I am indebted to Sarah Sutton for introducing me to these ideas.

interpretation of neuro-scientific findings. Some of his ideas are referenced in Daniel Stern's work, but it is specifically his ideas on 'insight' and 'regulation' that interest me.

I have already mentioned 'patterning at moments of improvisation' (a kind of – literally – insight, where I see something in a moment that was not previously visible – either because I could not see the pattern in previous experiences of similar moments, or because there is something about my experience of this particular moment which meant that I could act as if the pattern could be seen – by me, by us).

The literature on innovation abounds with examples of 'insight[58]' – indeed it sometimes seems as if the 'insight', the moment of insight is the (moment of) innovation. A typical (and inspiring) instance of this is described in *The Idea Book*[59] where Fredrik Härén describes how a group of designers, who were meeting in a desert location, got stuck; and both mentally and literally explored their environment. They learnt about the 'sidewinder' snake which detects its prey through heat seeking glands and nerves (the particularity of which lay in hunting at night where daylight vision would be of little value, yet where the desert is relatively cold, and therefore heat seeking is relatively sensitive; they were able to differentiate the body heat of prey against the cold background.)

---

58. For example, *The Idea Book* ; and Ken Robinson's *The Element; and How to Have Kick Ass Ideas* by Chris Barez Brown www.uppingyourelvis.com.

59. Published by www.interesting.org.

This led to the association of missile systems with heat seeking, which led to the insight that a heat seeking missile could be developed that would 'lock onto' either heat from engines or buildings. This led to the development of technology that can fire a missile into a chimney, or that can follow a plane or vehicle on the move. One application of this technology was called the 'sidewinder', in tribute to the desert snake inspiration.

I want us to concentrate less on the 'insight' here, and more on the process of association, the way-of-being-intimate in a different way; the intimate relation in this instance being with the context (the desert, and a snake that is particular to it) and the meaning, the sense-made. So we see 'association' being used in two senses, here - association of meaning; and social association[60] (relating to one another in (potentially) different ways).

We will discuss this in more detail later in this section – where we explore (we associate with) the concept and practice of 'free association' and what it suggests about processes of innovation. But for the moment, I want to relate these details to one of the themes in Allan Schore's work.

---

60. It is no coincidence that oppressive government's control 'association' eg. the UK anti-terrorism legislation controls access to other people, or mobile phones, or the internet for anyone under a control order; in China today (2012), there is relative freedom of debate about politics, but there is zero tolerance of any political organising that is an alternative to the Communist Party. Conversely, the 2nd term election success for Obama was based on different forms of association (organising) between groups who had not previously been – however loosely – associated.

One of the 'paradigm shifts' that Schore discusses is that 'therapy changes minds and brains', the force of this coming from his investigation of the biological substrate of the human unconscious (parsing how the unconscious is not a 'thing', but that it is embodied; colouring in what epiphenomenon might mean). In this discussion, he makes the point (in the *Journal of Clinical Social Work* 2008) that the clinician's knowledge of and access to her right brain is critical to the science of the art of psychotherapy. He sums this up by saying, *'the model of clinical expertise is regulation, not insight*[61]*'*.

What can we make of this? I want to associate to this material, and make some suggestions. In my interpretation I wonder....

- if for an innovator (or for anyone in an innovative relation to themselves and others), she might need to have access to and knowledge of her right brain (not as half of her brain, but as a system within a system, dynamically connecting to itself and other parts of the system);

- if innovation is a way of describing one of the dynamic forces that changes both the mind, and the brain; when we 'make sense' our senses are making us;

- if this process of innovation (whilst not therapeutic in the strict sense) is modelled as much on (different) forms of regulation, as it is on insight (the killer-app, or the kick-ass idea);

---

61. My summary from his work – particularly the presentation to American Psychological Association (2009).

- if regulation tends to be outsourced to 3rd parties – the 'regulatory authorities' (both literal and metaphorical) – rather than seen (also) as a process of self-governance or mutual-governance;

- if, when innovation and regulation in either the outside world (like financial markets) or the relative inner world of you and I working together, gets out of synch, we end up in a mess: no one can tell what is happening, and association (as we mean it) begins to break down;

- if we link regulation of the kind I am seeking to understand with you with an infantile state, where a parent needs to regulate a child – we certainly seem to link creativity with child-like innocence (as well as with the regulation of self disciplined practice). Maybe, I am bedazzled by my insights, and neglect my need to regulate, and be regulated;

- if we tend to neglect the nuanced, searching, mutually defined (and mutually defining) process of meaning-making when thinking about innovation in favour of the bold, decisive, all-change-now version of events. Something about this dynamic inter-play gets played down; something central to the process of innovation gets treated as a by-product, or a side-effect. Perhaps, this very tendency to elude and evade needs me to innovate with you, since I am less likely to avoid what is central (to me, to this particular context) if we are working (intimately) together;

- if there is a re-defining of competition in this – something gentler and more hesitant, something rivalrous, but moving (shifting, flowing, felt)...I can't quite grasp it on my own; I can't quite innovate on my own.

INTER-SUBJECTIVE DYNAMICS

Insight – now- also comes from the 'in-the-moment-connection' between you and I.

In the *Present Moment*, Stern introduces the idea of the inter-subjective matrix in which a special type of present moment is involved – that in which we experience co-creation and sharing at a moment of inter-subjective contact. I am not doing justice to his whole argument, here, but this emphasis (from page 75 and 77) is relevant to us:

'Our nervous systems are constructed to be captured by the nervous systems of others, so that we can experience others as if from within their skin, as well as from within our own. A sort of direct feeling route into the other person is potentially open and we resonate with and participate in their experiences and they in ours'.

Again, I feel like asking you to pause and consider this series of statements, and the images they evoke. It is as if we create an inter-personal www – our own net, our own nets for mutual capture, within which feelings, intentions, ideas, associations swarm and shoal and flock. Stern goes on to describe other people who:

'...are not just other objects, but are immediately recognised as special kinds of objects, objects like us, available for sharing inner states. In fact, our minds naturally work to seek out the experiences

in others that we can resonate with. We naturally parse others' behaviour in terms of the inner states that we can grasp, feel, participate in and thus share'.

We are each others' special kinds of objects – partners in innovation – in which a constant process of co-created change is taking place. This is a vivid description of a context in which regulation and shared experience interplay – indeed the sharing (because of the process of mutual capture we identify above) is the form of regulation. And in our thesis, this type of regulation is one of the conditions under which innovation can be nourished.

To me, this brings to mind a dynamic process, which is close to a finely meshed process of mutation, as if the long stretches of evolutionary branching had been compacted into something differently invisible; not hard to apprehend because of the multi generational intervals from which it is composed, but because of the micro palpitations of adjustment-with-and-to-another from which any felt experience is made up. Yet, just as in evolution, it is the mistakes in replication which we make – the missed steps[62] – that generate the lasting change. This is not the co-creation of imitation or mimicry; but co-creation out of mixed feelings. I need to be 'disturbed' by you and you by me.

Stern goes on to conclude (*The Present Moment* page 77)....

---

62. This puts me in mind of the idea discussed earlier in this section, that 'culture' is based on an agreement around how we break-the-rules-round-here.

'When we put all this together, a certain inter-subjective world emerges. We no longer see our minds as so independent, separate and isolated. We are no longer the sole owners, masters and guardians of our subjectivity. The boundaries between self and others remain clear, but more permeable. In fact, a differentiated self is a condition of inter-subjectivity. Without it, there would be only fusion. We live surrounded by others' intentions, feelings and thoughts that interact with our own, so that what is ours and what belongs to others starts to break down'.

And Stern goes on to describe the inter-subjective matrix as what strikes me as the software of intimate innovation:

'Our intentions are modified or born in a shifting dialogue with the felt intentions of others. Our feelings are shaped by the intentions, thoughts and feelings of others. And our thoughts are co-created in dialogue, even when it is only with ourselves. In short, our mental life is co-created. This continuous co-creative dialogue with other minds is what I am calling the inter-subjective matrix.'

FREE ASSOCIATION

One of the great innovations of psychoanalysis - in the eyes of some, the greatest - was the 'technique' of 'free association[63]'. There might be something in what has been learnt about this largely therapeutic

---

63. I am drawing on the ideas of Christopher Bollas and Adam Phillips in thinking about this.

practice that helps to point up what we are trying to pin down. It strikes me as a special kind of improvisation.

Christopher Bollas has written widely about psychotherapy – to my knowledge, his interest has been in the dynamics of individuals' relating, rather than groups or organisations. But is has always struck me how to-the-point his ideas are when applied to group and organisational life.

Free association[64] is a fundamental piece of technology in psychoanalysis with its origins in the recognition that creative discovery – to some extent – depends on allowing ideas to rush in 'pell mell'. In his writings[65] Bollas explores some of the features of free association and the quality of experience generated in a process of free association:

- Some of the associations are dreamy – they act as a kind of consolation, a 'swaddling in', and as a 'swaddling by';

- Some of them are abrupt and challenging – often in the form of 'giving-me-a-good-talking-to';

- Some concern granting permissions, and invoking prohibitions.

Under the conditions of free association, I am free to associate. My associations are free. A kind of storm can take place, I could describe

---

64. en.wikipedia.org/wiki/Free_association_(psychology)
65. For example, *Vitality of Objects Exploring the Work of Christopher Bollas* (Sage 2002).

free association as a kind of 'brain storming' – having a storm in my brain, an episode, a relapse. Under such conditions, my internal objects are free (more free) to associate – same figure, different ground[66]; same ground, different figure; different figure, different ground.

My external objects are free(er) to be associated (by me), although of course constrained.

But association of any kind = a particular kind of organising, a particular kind of relating....where 'what if' is the case. As if we were trying to fully contemplate uncertainty as a law of nature (which of course it is, yet we act as if by having laws of nature this is less the case). By implication, there is no inhibition, any figure can relate to any other figure....and in any way, striking us as carrying any meaning. Adam Philips spells this out in *On Flirtation* (quoted in wikipedia):

'the radical nature of Freud's project is clear if one imagines what it would be like to live in a world in which everyone was able - had the capacity - to free-associate, to say whatever came into their mind at any given moment...like a collage'

And I would go on to suggest that in another sense of free association, this image of collage, or cacophony, or chorus, is

---

66. Idea from Gestalt psychology – used by Larry Herschorrn in his essay *The Primary Risk*, reprinted in Psychoanalytic Studies of Organisations (Contributions from the International Society for the Psychoanalytic Study of Organisations (ISPSO 2009).

also an image of encounter (such as might happen in a meeting place – a market – where we all have something to exchange). In organisational & systemic innovation the freedom of people to associate as well as their capacity to free associate is part of what creates the capacity for innovation. Diversity, and mutation relate to this dynamic. I have a kind of market place within me, as without; we have a kind of market place between us.

We will each have our fantasy of a preferred market place[67] – a souk as opposed to a department store; a country store as opposed to a street market. The reputed dynamism of city life – with all of its myriad associations and, in particular, their randomness – is another version of this 'internal market'. In some sense my inner, subjective life is analogous to an 'internal market'; and the insights of Stern's version of the inter-subjective matrix makes clear that there is a kind of 'internal' (mutual) market between us, too.

And there is a link between the dynamic of 'free association' in the expanded, market-place way that we are considering it and the principles of emergence. In his book *Emergence* (1992), Steven Johnson summarises these:

- More is different – in so far as proliferation widens connection and mutual connection is a kind of 'difference engine';

---

67. Harrison Owen's 'open space technology' being an instance of a learning marketplace. Hundreds of Open Space meetings have been documented (www.openspaceworld.org).

- Ignorance is useful – in so far as knowledge acts as much as a seeker after evidence for pre-conceived ideas, as if does a generator of insight;

- Encourage random encounters – in so far as random (or as we discuss it 'free') association generates new connections, links and possibilities;

- Look for patterns – in so far as patterns will be the first signs of new linkages making their mark in a given context;

- Pay attention to neighbours – since it is those that are adjacent or close that are the link to the random and distant;

- Requisite variety – in connection is the basis of the 'bloom' of emergent patterns, the harbinger of insight; and

- Densely inter-connected – as a manifestation of our notion of regulation (where the connectivity on the one hand provides a vehicle for the expression of governance, but on the other is the phenomenon which increase the likelihood of variety in combination). The density of connections creates the conditions for the system; and the latent potential for regulation.

So, in the absence of (relative) inhibition, I am allowing the future to be itself – we are not trying to make what is going to happen a version of what has happened: this is getting to be the heart of intimate innovation – resisting the tendency to rob the future of its capacity to surprise.

And in my associating, I can be surprised by what happens - at least at the level of linking ideas and images, memories, colours, moods, resemblances etc. I can re-relate myself to some of the fundamentals of my life (to my elements) through this process of free association, in itself a method for innovating - and innovate in relation to aspects of life which are intrinsically intimate. Bollas discusses how there can be risks in doing it on your own....because you miss your own blind spot, of course...

Repetition - or the risk of repetition - can be noticed by the other – the blind spot spotter – repetition being counter-innovative. I can come up with something new - especially if there is someone else there – (usually a therapist in the pure version of free association).

It is fundamental to free associating that there is an 'observer' or 'audience' – indeed, the observer/audience is one of the processes at play as the emergent properties of the complex system become evident, the observer in making their observations 'intervenes' in the system.

But in wider systems of organising – wider that is than therapy – 'some-one-other' increasingly plays their part. This 'some-one-other' could be

- someone in a 'consulting stance'
- customers and consumers (as is the case in trans-media immersion)
- competitors
- partners.

This 'other' ensures that I am less likely to repeat myself, or at least use the latent, potential meaning in an association to simply confirm my status quo. This opens up the potential for innovation.

MY INTERNAL MARKETPLACE

It is thought-provoking to consider that here is *a kind-of-market-in-me* – my own 'internal market'. There is constant 'trading' going on in this place – there is bustle – there are gluts, and shortages – there is discounting and over pricing – there are supply chains – and so on and so on; and – like markets for nomads – this market has a habit of coming into being in certain settings, episodically – like the Kashgar market on Sunday, or a car boot sale.

Everything is connected in this internal market, although the connections may not be visible to me. The connections run through and with other people – and the versions of other people which is my experience of them. This is an intra-personal equivalent of the Medici Effect.

This market is immersive[68] - it involves a blurring of the transactions. Frank Rose (in his book, *The Art of Immersion*) provides an overview of immersive narrative. He writes:

'Not long ago we were spectators, passive consumers of mass media. Now, on YouTube and blogs and Facebook and Twitter, we are

---

68. See *The Art of Immersion: How the Digital generation is re-making Hollywood and Madison Avenue and the way we tell stories* (Frank Rose 2011).

media. And we approach television shows, movies, even advertising as invitations to participate—as experiences to immerse ourselves in at will.

'What we're witnessing is the emergence of a new form of narrative that's native to the Internet. Told through many media at once in a nonlinear fashion, these new narratives encourage us not merely to watch but to participate, often engaging us in the same way that games do. This is "deep media": stories that are not just entertaining but immersive, that take you deeper than an hour-long TV drama or a two-hour movie or a 30-second spot will permit.

From this point forward, storytellers of every persuasion will need to function in a world in which distinctions that were clear throughout the industrial age are becoming increasingly blurred:

- The blurring of author and audience: Whose story is it?
- The blurring of story and game: How do you engage with it?
- The blurring of entertainment and marketing: What function does it serve?
- The blurring of fiction and reality: Where does one end and the other begin?'

The context for these remarks is partiular – to do with trans-media story telling, especially on the Internet; but the content is closely related to our's. We can adapt his language, and pose similar types of questions, prompted by the blurring of the innovator and the adopter:

- whose innovation is it?
- how do you engage with it?
- where does my mind begin and your mind end when we are innovating?
- to what extent do we need to immerse ourselves in order to innovate?

The 'trades' and the 'exchanges' in this internal marketplace involve micro connectivity; they involve warmth & confrontation. They are meetings in which we meet one another – where we each have a take (an angle, a form of understanding) and where we take on one another (we push back and reciprocate).

These trades and exchanges are based on disturbance amongst and between equals. And for them to perpetuate, for them to carry on.... they have to be between equals, since it is only between equals that the disturbance of constant disequilibrium can be maintained. When I get stuck, I have lost my capacity for constant disequilibrium.

And in this internal market place, there are risks - risks (for example) of repeating patterns, of resorting to my own version of 'insider trading' – I can have a huge variety of real, present experiences with other people, yet respond to them as if they were mere confirmations of some pattern I knew would be demonstrated anyway – lapsing into 'getting my own back' – a 'species of revenge' – 'I told you so'....this exactly describes those conditions under which innovation is highly unlikely. Far from developing the capacity to change my mind, I am shoring up my own status-quo.

Surprise is important – there is a risk that my valency will shut down the possibility of surprise and re-inforce the particular ways in which I comply. In this way, I cut off my internal market from the rest of the world. My market goes into decline.

Surprise can help with noticing emergent patterns – especially at moments of improvisation, helping me to make sense in the moment – in ways which are nuanced, searching, mutually defined etc.

In order for it to flourish, my intimate innovation depends on a series of market conditions in my internal market, in which regulation is as significant (if not more significant) than insight; and...which is a zone in which something dissolves and re-combines; it is extensive, unbounded, yet sufficiently inhibited to become intelligible.

It can involve the emergence of a new agenda where I am the agenda – where I have to attend to my own intra-subjectivity in order to have the capacity to attend to the dis-orientating possibilities of being involved intimately with a specific context, or experience. And viewed in this way, you are as much of the context as the environment is.

There is a further risk – that of collapse into narcissism, where the only ideas worth having are *my* own. Our intimacy creates the elemental conditions for innovation.

The challenge of innovation – the innovation of challenge
The challenge of intimacy – the intimacy of challenge
Perhaps intimacy is *the* challenge of innovation...
Perhaps innovation is the challenge of intimacy

Birmingham
Nantucket
Malaga
Zennor
Birmingham

2011 – 2013

To find out more visit
www.intimate-innovation.co.uk

www.ingramcontent.com/pod-product-compliance
Ingram Content Group UK Ltd.
Pitfield, Milton Keynes, MK11 3LW, UK
UKHW042002230426
12048UKWH00009B/502